W9-ABO-063

Lionello Venturi | *Italian Painters of Today*

translated by Dorothy Cater

1959

LIONELLO VENTURI

Italian painters of today

UNIVERSE BOOKS, INC.

Cover and layout by Valeria Sissa

© DE LUCA EDITORE, 1959

Library of Congress Catalog Card No. 59-11871

Printed in Italy

PIRANDELLO

MAFAI

BIROLLI

SANTOMASO

CORPORA

AFRO

CASSINARI

TURCATO

SCIALOJA

SCORDIA

VEDOVA

PAINTERS OF TODAY

It is at once easier and more difficult to discuss painters living today than it is to comment on artists of the past. It is easier because one can follow the rhythm of their production, year by year and month by month, and one can listen to them voice their particular ideas. Sharing their life as artists is an essential requisite to an understanding of their art. As a witness of their worth one becomes more than a critic. On the other hand there is no tradition on which to found one's judgment of a contemporary painter, and it is part of the critic's task to establish such a tradition. It is easy to recognize that Piero della Francesca is a great artist. It is more difficult to choose among thousands of living painters those few who deserve to be remembered by posterity. It requires critical intuition; a quality rather hard to find. Although errors of judgment are inevitable, risks are worth taking, even for an understanding of the art of the past.

It has been said with authority that in order to comprehend a work of art a critic must begin with its subject and then define how this subject has been treated, that is to say, the image that the artist has made of it. It is on account of just this conception of history of art that a confusion has arisen between the subject and the content of the work, with the result that it is the culture rather than the creative personality of the artist which is described. The School of Athens *as a subject differs from the* Dispute of the Holy Sacrament, *but the content of both works, Raphael's approach, does not change with the change of subject; on the contrary it remains constant, even when it develops as the years pass.*

It has been said over and over again that the artist expresses himself, but it has not been recognized that the subjects chosen or accepted as commissions are all marginal to the artist's own expression. If the best artists of today have given up subjects, this is due to the greater aesthetic awareness they have compared to their predecessors. But while refusing subjects they have not renounced content, which would imply resigning oneself to non-existence. Many painters and sculptors present lines, forms and colors without any content because they are not true artists; but even realists, even illustrators of great and famous subjects, are "empty" unless they are artists. The presence or absence of subject does not condition the quality of a work of art.

The essential task of the critic who wishes to understand non-representational art, painting without subject, is to insist on content. In the past historical paintings, portraits, landscapes, still life, were material realities; they drew attention in centrifugal directions. The critic of today must concentrate his attention on the painter's way of feeling and thinking, on his manner of being. Only thus can he distinguish the true artist from the false and easily discover unity of form and content without leaning on the judgment of others or resorting to preconceived ideas.

The painters that are discussed in the following pages belong to the halfway generation. The oldest one, Pirandello, is sixty, and the youngest, Vedova, forty. Although some of them, especially Mafai, had reached concrete results even before the last war, it is unquestionable that they are famous today for the style they developed after the Liberation in 1945. Even those who opposed the taste that dominated during the Fascist period, even those who rebelled most violently against it, such as Birolli, Turcato or Vedova, felt themselves for that very reason in a hostile atmosphere, so hampered by restrictions that they were unable to give free rein to their imagination. They realized that an aesthetic autarchy was monstrous at a period when people had begun to recognize that the greatest artistic, intellectual, and social values were international. They knew all this, but in the tight enclosure where they lived it was difficult to understand what was being done abroad and hence to determine the direction best suited to their own nature.

After the Liberation they were able to say what they chose, and even if they were Communists they paid no attention to party orders. Not one of these eleven painters took part in the neo-realist movement. On the contrary, they displayed a desire to free themselves from the representation of natural objects and to express their imagination through lines, forms and colors. Each one of them has thus shown a preference for colors and forms with a varying emphasis on abstraction. Since each of these artists has now reached the height of his powers, I will attempt to comment on them in separate chapters.

At this juncture I would like to mention the points they have in common, the role they play in the artistic life of Italy today, and the reaction to their art outside Italy.

The use of abstract forms is what these artists have in common; some of them, like Turcato or Vedova rely completely or almost completely on abstractions as a means of expression; others instead, such as Pirandello, Mafai, Cassinari or Scordia, retain allusions and real images, even though their images are composed within the architecture of abstraction. These eleven painters are of today and they fulfil the criteria of contemporary pictorial taste because of the emphasis they place on abstraction. From the invention of Cubism onwards, a pervasive need has arisen to use line, form and color for expressing one's particular feeling or, better, one's being, beyond the representation of physical objects. The older generation can perfectly easily avoid such demands, even though Giorgio Morandi, with his little bottles, decries the value of the subject and expresses his own spirit rather than that of the little bottles in ineffably charming forms and colors — for which the bottles serve merely as a pretext. The best artists of the younger generations, however, have all aspired to abstraction, and not in Italy alone. A new international language has developed that is not difficult to understand if preconceived ideas do not arise to blur one's sight. When one stands in front of a painting by Turcato it is useless to ask what the subject is. Of course, such a painting represents a flight of the imagination, but imagination is not a tangible thing. The lines, forms, colors and motion represent the artist's spiritual life, his desires, his generosity, his grace. And if Turcato can convey such qualities it would be idiotic to ask him to portray so much as an apple.

If painters express their approach through lines, forms and colors, one wonders why most of them feel the need for pictorial allusions to real objects. It must be realized that for all of them impressions received directly from nature are the starting point for every painting. Even Mondrian, who has pushed his abstractions to the utmost limit, started with a natural vision of things. Afro waits for memory to bring back to his present life visions of times past, but their origin is in ordinary experience. In this process of transformation from natural reality to poetic vision, allusive forms may survive provided they are in harmony with abstract forms. They constitute neither an advantage nor a disadvantage; all that counts is the final result.

It is well known that formal abstract painting arose out of Cubism from which all other non-representational forms are derived, of which the most radical and extreme were invented by Kandinsky first and, later on, by Mondrian. The revival of abstract painting, when it had fallen into disrepute and seemed about to die out, was the work of a group of young painters who, in 1942, rebelled in their own way against the German oppression by holding an exhibition in Paris entitled Peintres de tradition française. *Their leader was Bazaine, and he gathered around him Manessier, Tal Coat, Estève, Lapicque, and others. They attempted to produce concrete effects, of a spiritual nature, by means of abstract forms. For this reason they were called abstract realists. Their art is very refined; no one better than Bazaine can create new color harmonies, full of feeling and sensibility. No one better than Manessier succeeds in expressing mystic contemplation by weaving together pure lines. If the French abstract realists have a limitation, it is their ultra refinement, their great tradition which perhaps restricts their scope unduly.*

The more progressive artists, those who represent the avant-garde of our period and who are ready to break completely with every tradition and fling open the doors to the future, are some American painters, such as Pollock, Tobey, Gorky, De Kooning, etc. Their tradition is limited, but it has not prevented them from understanding that pictorial matière itself can supply poetic meaning. It was necessary to create a pictorial matière that would contain the spiritual values of artists. Pollock certainly succeeded in doing this and others besides, with a greater or lesser degree of freedom. One can stress the fact that the positive and practical American attitude has found its highest expression not in an idealistic flight but in the concrete essence of the matière itself.

The most successful and internationally popular abstract realists are Italian painters. They are less radical than the Americans, less refined than the French, but they have great qualities; they are enthusiastic, spontaneous, daring, they feel a constant need to renew themselves and, finally, they have something which is theirs alone, natural facility for painting. International success has given them the responsibility of avoiding repetition, of not permitting themselves to become mannered copyists of their own style even if they feel that its further development should be consistent with earlier work. In other words, they have a vitality that cannot be explained but which exists and in which their strength lies.

At no time in our century has the success of Italian painting been as great as it is today, thanks, above all, to the work of those eleven painters that will be discussed in this commentary. These painters are recognized as Italian artists, not because they are bound to local century old traditions, but because they express international ideals in an Italian way. Our national artists are, in fact, not those who follow academic traditions but Italians who paint according to their own particular bent.

The most frequent objection raised against painters and sculptors who adopt abstract forms wholly or in part is that they fail to fulfil their traditional task of creating images of men or women, landscapes or still life. In reply to this objection I have for years cited the fact that architects represent neither men nor apples, but that they nevertheless succeed —and how well— in giving expression to their imagination through form and color. And since it is well known that no aesthetic system exists which denies painting those privileges allowed architecture, painters can reach the highest artistic levels without representing anything whatsoever. There is, however, another objection which I must deal with. Modern civilization is not a civilization of "élites." Democracy has taken the place of the ancient aristocracy. Anyone working for a restricted class cannot feel in harmony with the tendencies of modern civilization. The new arts of cinema and television either please the masses or cease to exist. This is why Communist leaders invented Neo-realism, the only style, even in painting, that could be understood by the masses and could thereby inspire works of art to suit present tastes.

And it is just because the Communists believed they had solved the problem by pushing it to its extreme consequences that one may see the effects of this solution. Not only was the artistic level of the Russian pavilion at the 1956 and 1958 Venetian Biennales unbearably low, but also those Italians who adhered to Neo-realism ruined themselves and lost such qualities as they might have formerly possessed. On the other hand, as soon as the severity of the neo-realistic dictatorship decreased, abstraction reappeared in Poland, for instance, and even in Czechoslovakia and in Russia itself, so one hears. This "pleasing the people" which kills art is therefore an extremely odd necessity, in that both artists and the people themselves reject it as soon as they are able.

On the other hand, in countries where there is freedom of opinion and where abstract art flourishes, who condemns it? The archaeologists who, as schoolboys, were taught to consider Greek art as eternal and absolute perfection and who refuse to admit that art today can be conceived in any other way than the only one they have known previously. The Vatican authorities that imagine people's faith is on the same level of sentimentality as the oleographic pictures used to decorate altars, and who believe that their taste is the authorized continuation of Renaissance and Baroque art. Other enemies of abstraction are those ultra-refined writers who need to feel superior to everybody else, to individuals as well as to groups in order to prove something to themselves. In the same way a few big businessmen prefer to collect ancient art. They are surrounded by the instruments of modern life, from the telewriter to nuclear energy all day long, but when they think of art they wish to escape from their daily round. This romantic attitude shows that they practice a profession which brings them profit but which they neither love nor estimate at its true value, since other-

wise they would search for the type of art most in keeping with their profession and expressive of their own way of life.

Neither archaeologists, nor the Vatican authorities, nor those ultra-refined writers, nor any of the big businessmen appreciate modern art, abstract or otherwise. They live in the past, with the illusion that it continues unchanged in the present.

Think, instead, of the young people of today who have not been ruined by a classical education. They look with pleasure at this weaving of lines and colors without demanding what is represented. Look at the children who draw according to their inspiration and not according to their teachers' wishes. Some of them tell stories and are illustrators but others, who as the saying goes "draw for beauty", create abstract patterns.

It is odd that this art which comes spontaneously to children and pleases young people should be accused of being a sealed book suitable only for initiates. A taste for the abstract is developing not only in the field of architecture but also in decoration, in every-day objects, in clothing. But from painting and sculpture, from great art, abstraction must be banned!

When a proposal was made to set up a monument to Dante in Rome, public reaction was so violent that the proposal had to be withdrawn. What caused this reaction? A bronze or marble figure in the center of a public square is unthinkable in modern times, and ridiculous as well. It is already difficult for us to put up with the many statues that were erected in the nineteenth century. A piece of architecture in honor of Dante would have solved the problem. Nobody will admit it but the fact is that direct representation of human beings no longer pleases anyone; and if anybody wants a portrait, let him go to a photographer.

All this upsets the feelings of many people who are still attached to the classic or humanist conception of life: honorable conceptions that have given great and glorious results, but that belong to the past. Why should this be? If I were to select the outstanding characteristic of classicism and humanism, I would say it consists in the interrelationship of man and nature. Even then nature was used for man's advantage, it was transfigured, but it still remained nature. The quality of spirit, as opposed to matter, was recognized as belonging to man alone. An equilibrium of spirit and of matter was necessary in art as in science; man and nature continued to be interrelated.

Then came the philosophers who, with greater or lesser imagination, told us that everything was spirit and that matter was absorbed by the spirit. Only the experts adopted this idea, because public opinion ridiculed them. Then came the scientists who not only say that matter is merely energy, but even use this energy which can neither be seen nor felt, and which no one understands, but which allows itself to perform prodigies of good and evil. From the discovery of that unknown which is called electricity to the everyday use of nuclear

14

energy, man invents, creates and transforms to suit himself what he supposes to exist, but which has no body and is not an object and is not separated from his mind. The interrelationship with nature of the classic and humanist age is over, and is no longer of use except for moments of repose and inactivity.

Modern man, the man of today, speaks with himself and in so doing creates that world of his own which suffices for life, for thought, and for desire. Is it not natural that under such conditions even the imagination prefers soliloquy, and does not require nature, in which no one believes, to express itself? If, as it seems to me, this is the reason for abstract art, this art fulfils the needs of civilization today, that is, of all men and women who effectively live their lives in the present. Little by little, people who belong to past civilizations will disappear, even if they are not aware of it.

In this way abstract art, rather than being a sealed book to all but small select coteries, offers the enjoyment of form and color to everyone, regardless of social status.

Other consequences of this state of affairs are reflected in the artistic character of the works produced. Above all the artists are no longer interested in the plastic consistency of the forms, but prefer revelations in color with lesser emphasis on reasoning but greater freedom of imagination.

Furthermore, completion of the pattern, with a center around which everything takes place, is no longer necessary. It was necessary when a work of art was something detached from the world, when it was a world in itself. All one asks of a painting today is that it should give us a moment of creative pleasure in a rhythm that can continue to infinity.

At one time it was believed that form, produced by chiaroscuro, was correlated to man's thought, and color to his senses. Today it is realized that colors adapt themselves with greater ease and freedom to an artist's imagination. They suggest space, but follow more naturally the rhythm of time to which we let ourselves go as if to something within ourselves rather than to something outside us, such as space. If today, therefore, some painters employ forms and colors that do not represent natural objects it is not a caprice, as ignorant people believe, but fate, our historical fate which holds in store for us great hardships but also infinite joy.

L. V.

PIRANDELLO

FAUSTO PIRANDELLO

I do not claim to have discovered Fausto Pirandello. He obtained recognition on his own some considerable time ago. Furthermore, the writings of Virgilio Guzzi, Roberto Melli, Emilio Cecchi, Mario Soldati and Libero De Libero have helped to clarify various aspects of his art. But I hope that I, too, can succeed in explaining some aspects.

Pirandello's isolation has been stressed. As a man he has been isolated in the past, today luckily rather less so, since in recent years the public, collectors, and art juries have begun to understand him. But as an artist he is spontaneous and sincere and not in the least isolated. He has said of himself: "I realize that I don't succeed in checking the impulse of doing what I do as best I can; whether that be well or ill." I emphasize the humility of this phrase and at the same time his sense of duty towards himself that it reaffirms implicitly. It would seem as if he wished to finish his statement with "Così è, se vi pare", the words of his great father from whom he took more than a spiritual attitude, even if he has painted for himself and for the few rather than for the many. And it should be strongly emphasized that the greatness and infinite daring of modern painting made this an obligation for him. As an artist he is therefore isolated as are all the true artists today.

The most one can allow is that his imagination lacks some of that cordial quality which other painters possess and which eases their relationship with others. For a long

18

PLATE 1

Paesaggio, 1954, De Luca Collection, Rome

time Fausto was not a lucky man, and he suffered because he was unwilling to make concessions. The nature of his artistic temperament is shown by the very fact that he would perhaps have liked to make concessions but did not succeed in doing so. From this stems an undeniably pessimistic attitude towards mankind, borne fatalistically, which provokes atrocious sarcasms but also results in his being surprised and moved when he discovers a gleam of beauty or goodness in the evil mass of humanity.

Some writers have tried to interpret Pirandello's apparent isolation in such a way as to make him a champion of their nationalistic ideas. Nothing could be less accurate. It should be stressed that the school to which Pirandello belonged and still belongs is the European school. If he felt isolated in Rome between 1932 and 1939, this was only due to the fact that in Rome one was isolated from the world, but he did not deliberately isolate himself. He has had a better education than most painters, and one gets the definite impression from the little he has written that he is a hardy logician. But when he paints, he is seldom governed by his intellect; he is sensual, even to a fault, passion overwhelms both the man and the images he creates. For these reasons he is a strong colorist and the least intellectual among the colorists; his best results come when he uses color to create his form.

I have never seen any of the works that Fausto Pirandello painted before he went to Paris in 1928. He was born in Rome in 1899 and went to secondary schools in that city; in 1917 he was called up for military service. He began to paint without attending the Academy and exhibited at the 1926 Biennale, but he has refused to preserve any works of that period, which he considers technically immature.

In the meantime he had been affected by Van Gogh, through reproductions, and had seen the works of Carrà and Carena. He had never heard of Morandi.

In Paris he fell in love with Cézanne, with the volume of his forms, with his still lifes. Like most painters at that time, however, he did not see the chromatic and impressionistic basis of Cézanne's forms. Thus, for this reason, his imitations of Cézanne were limited, careful and objective, without poetic flights. In Paris, however, he overcame the tyranny of subject in favor of compositions based on the inner necessities of mass and tone, subordinating completion of the object portrayed to the exigencies of the composition.

His *Tondi* in the Vallone Collection, Rome, is a typical example of his style in the years 1928-31. *Bottigliette*, in the Laudisa Collection, Rome, of the same period, is even finer because its light and color are more sensitive, in spite of the use of coarse tints, low in tone. The cardboard box is yellow and light blue; it isolates the transparency of the bottles, painted in gray. Since Morandi's painting was unknown

PLATE 2

Paesaggio, 1958

to him, the obvious affinity of subject can be explained by the historical problems of that period, which affected them in a similar manner.

He also painted some landscapes and views of the city in the same style as his *Bottigliette*. He exhibited at the Vildrac Gallery on the rue de Seine and was in touch with everything that was being done in Paris at that time. Picasso's paintings fascinated him, but it never occurred to him to imitate them because, as he now says, "I didn't understand the simultaneous vision of space and time."

And now for an aspect of Pirandello's character that should be stressed. His sentimental reactions can be sudden and violent, but where his art is involved he moves cautiously. In recent times he has become daring, but he waited until he felt sure of himself.

On returning to Rome in 1931 he was discouraged by the feeling of stagnancy, the generally oppressive atmosphere; he attempted vainly to adapt himself to the realistic and thematic painting imposed by the Fascist regime. His temperament, or his good fortune, forced him into passive resistance. He does not seem to have been affected either by Scipione or by Mafai.

Ritratto della suocera in the Natale Collection, Rome, and the *Donna e bambino*, in a private collection, both of which date from 1931, display his gift for synthesis and tonal composition. Critics have given a certain acclaim to his *Interno del mattino*, 1932, which would be beautiful were the plastic modelling of the woman in the foreground in harmony with the rest of the painting.

In the meantime Fausto's color had become thick and pulpy and, although less intense, well blended and capable of creating form, when his modelling did not destroy the effect. But light, as atmosphere enveloping color, did not interest the painter. An exception to this is his painting *Tre Donne*, 1939, in the De Luca Collection, Rome, where light filters on to the figures from above. The colors lose their brightness and fade away; at that time light was only used to give animation to the matière.

Then came the war; the Pirandello family went to live in the country and there the painter worked by himself at refining his tonal values. *Le ventole*, 1944, in the Laudisa Collection, Rome, is perhaps his masterpiece of that period. There is a sarcastic aim that is not expressed by any one object but in the sharpened attention paid to the rhetorical matière of the red damask and the white paper as a contrast to the poor, worn-out fans. This symbolic value is felt in the matière of the pigment but there is no proof of its existence.

Contadino piccolo, where the form dissolves to intensify the vitality of the image, dates from 1943, not from 1946, as has been stated elsewhere.

After the Liberation Pirandello understood the new values that a simultaneous vision of space and time can give, thanks to the new emotional climate that had arisen and the exhibits of works by major living artists, and also through the spontaneous attainment of inner maturity. He has discovered a new horizon, towards which he will march with his usual caution, that is to say, without ever losing his perception of exterior aspects of objects.

Some first-rate paintings of this period are the *Natura morta con falce*, 1950, in the Bloc Collection, Rome, *Natura morta*, 1950, in the National Gallery of Modern Art, Rome, *Il Flauto*, 1947, in the Civic Museum of Turin, and *Le Note Grandi*, also of

Plate 3   *Mito,* 1954

1947, in the De Luca Collection, Rome. Perhaps the finest of all the foregoing is *Tavolino da tè*, 1953, in the Perina Collection, Rome. Its color is so pure it need not be extremely bright in order to burst into song.

Pirandello's recent still lifes reveal a perception of reality arising from chaos, as it were; the effect is of a thing created parallel to natural reality but distant from it because it is the reality of art and full of art's pleasing qualities.

In order to obtain similar effects with the human figure certain distortions are required that the public accepts less willingly. In this field Pirandello has only gradually become sure of himself. Whereas in *Antonio in viola*, 1947, in the Estorick Collection, London, there is still a feeling of effort, in *Bagnanti al pesce*, 1949, in a private collection, the image has become more organic.

But in *Nudo*, 1953, which won the Marzotto Prize and is in Count Marzotto's Collection, Valdagno, everything is just as it should be. By this I mean that not a brush stroke nor a tone is used that cannot be justified by the existence of the created form. The blacks and the reds are violent, and expressive accents, rather than conventional chiaroscuro, create a spontaneous effect of plasticity.

This work is the first in a new cycle of figures; Pirandello painted several that have a similar inspiration. One example of this cycle is *Figura preoccupata*, in the Venice Gallery of Modern Art, painted in 1954 and where his quadrilaterals of color and his will to bring the figure to the surface are much more evident than in his 1953 *Nudo*. The use of quadrilaterals gives an expansive and vital quality to the color. It should be noted that the color of his still lifes is lighter, more airy and delicate than in his figures. Could this be because his freedom of expression, the fruit of much labor, allows him to stress his sarcastic and pessimistic attitude towards human nature? Whatever the reason, the development of his style can be traced by studying the woman with the sunflower, to which he gives the title *Mito*, 1954 (Plate 3), where the formal rhythm already overcomes the violence of expression and where the color harmony becomes natural.

In *Bagnanti*, 1956, (Plate 4) he merely makes a gesture towards representation, in order to establish a rhythm of lines and areas of abstract color, although he does so with his usual vibrant sensibility.

Pirandello's landscapes are the best key to his evolution during the past ten years. One of these, *Campagna a Riofreddo*, in the Lucherini Collection, Rome, shows a synthesis of volumes and a desire to construct that derives from Cézanne but to which Fausto adds his nervous and tormented personal touch, interpreting Cézanne after the manner of Van Gogh. In *Tetti di Roma*, 1944, in De Luca Collection, Rome, a quieter painting, there are hints of the influence of the Roman tonal school on Pirandello. In a landscape of 1954 in the De Luca Collection, Rome, (Plate 1) he shows, on the other hand, the impact of various new experiences that go from cubist abstraction to the

24

PLATE 4   *Bagnanti,* 1956

PLATE 5   *Limoni*, 1957 Marino Collection, Milan

Kokoschka type of Expressionism, but which yield new and unexpected results. These show themselves in a greater leaning towards synthesis and at the same time a yielding to nature—abstraction that tends towards the concrete and above all towards the grandiose, like a force of nature. The main colors are gradations from green to yellow, enough to give a sensation of the richness of color and sharpness of the planes. It is as if nature were undergoing an upheaval involving everthing except the sky. Not even landscape painting brings tranquillity to this painter.

PLATE 6

Biscotti e liquori, 1957

In *Pergola e pini*, another painting of 1954, formal organization prevails over the representation of nature, as if the latter were painted from two points of view and with a heavy accent on the architectural elements.

Platani e peri, 1956, is an organic composition, where greens and yellows are used to give an impression of space and of imaginary perspectives. The manner of applying color to the surface conveys perfectly this sense of space. Pirandello stresses this style with great coherence in his *Paesaggio*, 1958, (Plate 2) where abstraction is more severe and the subject is blended with the background, giving a fantastic architectural effect, as if he could simultaneously see the plan of a city and its elevation.

It is interesting to follow the development of his still lifes from the study of the model to the final formal effect. *Libro verde* is a study from the model, but the model is so complicated that it answers the demands of the most stringent formality. To begin with, the chair is set aslant to occupy space and the dishes seem to leap through the surface of the painting, then the glass and the book serve to supply an area of formal repose and of pleasing color between the foreground and the background. A feeling of exceptional plastic energy springs from this confusion.

Different aspects of Pirandello's imagination can be seen in two works of 1957. *Limoni* (Plate 5) inserts objects into real space, thus giving them a degree of material consistency. *Biscotti e liquori*, (Plate 6), that won the Fiorino Prize, on the other hand, shows a series of bevelled areas that imply a loving study of real objects but rises above them with poetic inspiration. The painting does not merely show us bottles and biscuits. It conveys the spirit of a party, confusion, excitement expressed in an unequalled manner... a moment of life caught in lines and colors... Pirandello has finally freed himself from the bondage of imitation.

In developing his style Pirandello followed the slow, gradual, and painful process of detaching himself from the object represented with the aim of obtaining complete coherence in form and color; in so doing he did not renounce his goal of revealing nature's essence through the use of abstract form.

MAFAI

MARIO MAFAI

More than once I have asked myself why Mario Mafai is not as celebrated and famous in Italy as the best painters of the last half century. In 1930, when he exhibited with Scipione, Libero De Libero, a very young poet, acclaimed him for reviving painting when it had lost all its vitality. The curious thing is that later on no one ever doubted, indeed everybody recognized that Mafai represented the true current in Roman painting, and it was believed that a Roman school had been founded by him although he never had the wish to found a school. This factor, perhaps, has restricted the development of his art to a Roman ambience, and thus detracted from his reputation.

After his early successes and when he had to carry on alone after the death of his friend Scipione, Mafai succeeded in finding a correlation between his form and the subject-content in such paintings as *Fiori secchi* or *Demolizioni*. Giorgio Morandi had already attained this correlation, which perhaps no other painter in Italy (De Pisis lived abroad) had reached at that time

The horrors of war had the effect of making Mafai turn towards ferocious satire and cling to this approach.

Although he never was drawn to the neo-realists, after the Liberation he depicted houses and people in a calm, leisurely and unharried way, he seemed too little involved. Finally, in the most recent works of his that I have seen, it is hard to decide whether they are more abstract or more concrete, but he seems to have reached a solution of his own

PLATE 7

San Lorenzo, 1945 De Luca Collection, Rome

to the problems which harass all painters. He solves them through naturalness barely heightened by the audacity of an actor improvising a role. He replied to my query as to why he had changed his style during the past few months, "Because I was tired of painting the old way," a reply evoking despair or exaltation according to one's choice of aesthetic.

Mafai's culture is wide and on a high level, although a certain plebeian coarseness and typically Roman irony hide it well, characteristics that have certainly not enhanced the artist's reputation, even though they may have helped him artistically. His ways have perhaps cramped his scope, but they have obliged him to remain concerned with pictorial problems and to avoid literary red herrings. Besides this, although he is of course loath to show it, his moral sense is highly developed; when malicious fun is poked at some fellow painter, one looks around the circle after the laughter dies down and finds that Mafai has disappeared.

His friendship with Scipione has been the only one in his whole life so far, as he himself says, "The kind of friendship that no longer exists." It is evident that Scipione's exceptional powers of imagination helped Mafai and made him feel the need for a lyrical culture, of aspiration beyond reality, and of freedom from every school. After Scipione's death an idle tale arose that it was Mafai who had gained the most benefit from their friendship, and only in recent years, through the work of some young researchers, has it been established that Scipione's particular pictorial qualities were inspired by his friend; and Mafai never made the slightest effort to correct this tale which was to his detriment. Shyness, diffidence and timidity are rather rare qualities today. But because Mafai has never had proper recognition, he feels alone in the world; perhaps this dates from the time he felt so lost after Scipione's death. "Then gradually I started on my way again, but this time entirely on my own."

The attitude he expressed in 1954 towards recent tendencies of contemporary art is typical of the man. "Abstract painting has been, and for some time to come will still be interesting, more from a polemical standpoint than for its inherent qualities. The polemical side, in my opinion, is the best one of this movement, it consists in the search for new formal possibilities, in a more precise use of technical means — color, line, space, and form. I would call it a healthy and useful academic exercise.

"Certain principles of Neo-realism are acceptable: its generous impulse, its invitation towards a more direct participation in life, its greater sympathy towards mankind; but unfortunately the sort of men neo-realists depict are nearly always rather ugly, unattractive — they never shave. Certainly if their canvasses showed fewer unshaven chins and more respect for painting there is little doubt that Neo-realism would make great strides." [1]

In 1954 Mafai was a Communist, but even that did not succeed in making him like ugly painting. He saw that abstract painting opened new vistas of form and color, but he did not feel it had sufficient content to produce a work of art. Today Mafai has learned to give content to his type of abstract painting. He has thus gone back to the fullness of expression of his *Fiori secchi*, of his *Demolizioni*, but with an infinitely broader style and with a creative ability purer than artistic reality.

[1] *Pittura d'oggi*, Vallecchi, Florence, 1954.

PLATE 8

Veduta romana, 1956 La Tartaruga Gallery, Rome

We can find distant traces in the artist's consciousness of his surrender to the color-space relationship beyond any concern with representation. He wrote in 1940, "My experiments began late, towards my thirtieth year. At that point I painted flowers in the sun. I placed them haphazardly, without any attempt at composition. I copied them one by one, and I realized that as they faded they created their own particular space, an abstract appearance, like that of certain people of whom one only recalls a gesture, high-flown or merely resigned. I painted and the color came out bright but chaste, and I was enchanted with those yellows and those scarlets.

"I put nudes, figures and objects in sunlight. These bodies in a gray and empty room developed their own space inside the walls, rich in sonorous vibrations, light and color. These experiments revealed to me the functions of space more and more clearly, and as a result they carried me towards wider concepts of construction and color." [2]

In 1942, after deploring the lack of interest painters had in the human form, Mafai

[2] *Tempo*, Milan, March 1940.

wrote: "The painter's enthusiasm is aroused by other forms: he is attracted to a different genre; he takes any object which can arouse vibrations and color and a feeling of space, such as an apple, material of some curious color, a piece of glass with its sparkle; all elements that make up the spectacular flora which feeds his imagination." [3]

Such are the spontaneous flights from a realistic ambience towards the enchanted world of fantasy which have kept Mafai young so that today he finds himself more in harmony with artists in their thirties than those in their fifties. His case may be unique; it is, at all events, an exemplary one.

Mario Mafai was born in Rome in 1902 and after attending technical and industrial schools he went on to the British School and the French Academy, to the free life-classes, the museums, and the library of the Institute of Archaeology and History of Art.

He first exhibited with Scipione in 1928, at Palazzo Doria, and then in the shows organized by the trade union of artists in 1929, 1930 and 1932. He exhibited at the first Quadriennale in 1931, and at the second in 1935; at the Venice Biennale Shows in 1934 and 1938 and in 1948 and 1958 when special rooms were set aside for him.

Mafai has always lived in Rome except for a year spent in Genoa in 1940; throughout his entire life his work has completely absorbed him.

In order to understand the origins of Mafai's art, I believe it is necessary to go beyond his friendship with Scipione, who doubtless thrust his friend towards unknown frontiers with an impetus and revolutionary force of conviction that must have been formidable. As a painter, however, Mafai has made his own way. Even the advice of Antonietta Raphael, who later became his wife, although it brought a timely whiff of internationalism into the lazy Roman ambience of 1929 and precious experience in the free use of color, was not much more than an instigation to look for something new.

Mafai's trip to Paris in 1930, on the other hand, should be given considerable importance in my opinion; his own account of it, with the title "La Pittura parigina", was published in the October 19, 1930 number of *Italia Letteraria*.

At that time it was more difficult to get one's bearings in Paris concerning French art than it is today since neither the Museum of Impressionist Painting nor that of Modern Art as yet existed. And this did in fact disconcert Mafai; he reacted unfavorably to the ambience. He believed that Picasso, Modigliani and Chagall owed nothing to France but that they had continued to paint in France as Spaniards, or Italians, or Russians. It is easier to understand that such ideas were an improvised defense mechanism against the danger of losing his own traits and being "condemned to orbit continually around one star or another."

[3] *Prospettive*, March 15, 1942, page 19.

PLATE 9   *Fiori*, 1957 Franchetti Collection, Rome

According to Mafai, internationalism in painting as it was practised in Paris was the result of a desire for applause, of a thirst for material awards. To this internationalism Mafai opposed his concept of universality, a synthesis of heaven and earth, not in the realistic sense but as an expression of sheer humanity. It was a utopian idea, because universality can only be found through international life, but an idea which sheds light on Mafai's idealistic tendencies as a young man.

When he heard Paris spoken of as "la ville de la contemplation" he refused to accept this definition. He thought of Paris as a city palpitating with life and gaiety, not a place for saints or mystics. He believed instead that Italian art "from the earliest Baroque period up to the eighteenth century had this feeling of enchantment, poetry and spirituality," and as far back as 1930 he dreamed of Italy's artistic leadership. He couldn't have lost his bearings more completely. He didn't understand the realities of the situation in which he found himself, but he expressed his spiritual demands. And it is these which are important. All the more so since, without realizing it, without admitting it even to himself, some of the Paris experience made itself felt in his painting. He says today that he admired Braque and Matisse but not Picasso when he was in Paris. At that time young Italian painters, such as Francesco Menzio, were atracted to the older French artists, Bonnard for instance, and it would seem from Mafai's earlier work that he too felt their influence. On the whole, the influence which Mafai seems to have felt most keenly is that of the symbolists, he shared with them a vague aspiration towards mysticism.

It is undeniable that his *Tre bambine nel giardino*, 1931-1932 [4], with its renunciation of volume and its lack of any facial delineation, shows more the influence of Pont Aven than of the Milanese Novecento school.

The same may be said of his *Nudi*, 1932 and of *Nudo con la Palla*. There is a certain shyness in the approach to form, of aristocratic and restrained elegance, a vitality in the brushwork that uses light to form the image, that has no precedent in the Italian tradition. Some precedent, although completely transformed, can be found in the French tradition, in Bonnard once again, perhaps also in Picasso of the pink period.

Mafai's dark mood of pessimism, as revealed by his letter from Paris, was destined to increase when he returned to his Roman circle. Some of the *Fiori* he did in 1932 are among his favorite subjects; faded, they droop to prevent one from seeing their further decay, as Mafai used to say or, as we think, in order not to reveal his own desperation. And meanwhile he created delicious linear rhythms. In 1938 he made other paintings of flowers, this time strewed on a page from Traviata. I can almost hear Mafai's ironic remarks about those who believe that there is some connection

[4] In L. De Libero's monograph on Mafai, published by De Luca in 1949, the reader may find the greater part of the paintings which are mentioned here but not reproduced.

between those flowers and the opera. In our opinion this painting is a masterpiece of light and shadow, delicate and complex, with purely visual values.

At the time when the construction of a greater Rome was being celebrated at the expense of the ancient and medieval city, Mafai heard a cry arising from those buildings being pulled down, from those anonymous dwellings, bits of life that were slipping away. Something worse than a faded flower, since nothing was left of the ancient life. Ever since the seventeenth century the ruins of Rome have attracted painters, and quenched the curiosity of tourists or increased a thirst for the knowledge of her past grandeurs. Nothing of this happened to Mafai. His *Demolizioni* feel the need to give life through light and shade even to the blow of the pick-axe. The *Demolizioni* of 1936 in the Rome Gallery of Modern Art and the *Demolizioni a via Ripetta* in the Gualino Collection, Rome, are two fine examples of these themes.

His *Fiori secchi* and his *Demolizioni* are the means of escape Mafai used in maturing his style. It is a style based on color that creates and justifies the form. And the function of the subject is to offer a pretext to form which through its variety, I might even say its casualness, allows color to undertake the task of guide. Critics have called this color "tonal" like the imaginary Roman school that is attributed to Mafai, but it has already been stated that if by "tone" one means the Venetian tone of the sixteenth century, the relationship between color, resonance, and light in Mafai is something quite different. But perhaps "tone" may mean any relationship between color and light, as much Giorgione's or Vermeer's as Renoir's. In this case, the relationship used by Mafai is certainly a kind of tone as well, obtained through contrast instead of through shading. He seems to harmonize his colors on the basis of their *timbre* which he loves and experiences, and only as an afterthought does he give them accompaniment which provides tonal support for the harmony. Naturally the contrast between the timbres of the colors and basic tone is attenuated because his reds are velvety, his greens contain no sunlight, and his violets are "vestment" shades — according to Marchiori —; thus Mafai's color is the color of Rome, just as Guardi's is that of Venice. But it is a Rome which fades out on the palette of the most Roman painter of them all since he does not need to seek Rome out, he lives in her midst.

Once Mafai's style had matured, he could draw on it for many subjects that were more or less of literary origin. Recollections of metaphysical painting, or nudes treated like dress models, such as *Indossatrici*, 1940, in the Asta Collection, Venice, or *Figura*, 1943, where there is much more realism in the brutality of the pose than in the way it is handled, and in *Figure distese*, 1937 and 1938, where a certain awkwardness of the pose conveys the meaning.

A perfect work is the *Ritratto di Fersen*, 1942, where the values are entirely spiritual because the style has completely fused the form.

During the war Mafai painted a series of bitter satires against human cruelty and brutality: *Interrogatorio, Conquistatori, I barbari, La vittoria, Marcia trionfale, Impiccati*, etc. *Caserma*, 1942, shows the moral and physical poverty of those soldiers who gave themselves the air of conquerors. The greater part of this war scenes wish to and succeed in expressing concentrated horrors, horrible deformations, and reach a pitch of the most unbridled bestiality.

Few artists are such masters of the human form as Mafai, of its movements, and fore-shortenings, but his drawing is naturally delicate and light, his lines are glancing but not cutting. The former quality enables Mafai to depict rainstorms, the second prevents all forms of violent expression. It seems that Mafai is too much of an artist to take to satire and also that reality of that time was too ferocious for him to face.

Mafai was living the factious life of his time when he was awarded the 1941 Bergamo Prize.

Once the war over the artist felt the need for his art to harmonize with the new kind of life and also for it to oppose the literary fetish for unintelligibility. When the "Fronte delle Arti" was set up, Mafai would not join it because it was too much of an abstract trend. And when Togliatti started Neo-realism, Mafai although a Communist, would not join that movement because he wanted his own kind of realism to be an artistic expression rather than a political one.

He tried new subjects — houses and roads in the suburbs, shopkeepers, inns, wide landscapes — with the object of lessening the descriptive side of representation and reducing forms to the essentials. We can well understand the difficulty of the immediate post-war situation. By now Mafai was bound to a very honorable past and his own temperament would not permit him to throw himself haphazardly into one of the two diverging paths along which younger painters were seeking their way. He himself says that Chanfort's suggestion is too often in his mind: "Un philosophe retiré du monde m'écrivait une lettre pleine de vertu et de raison. Elle finissait per les mots: 'Adieu, mon ami; conservez si vous pouvez les intérêts qui vous attachent à la société; mais cultivez les sentiments qui vous en séparent'." ("A philosopher who had retired from the world wrote me a letter full of fine principles and sound reasoning. It ended with these words: 'Good-bye my friend; retain, if you can, those interests which bind you to society, but cultivate those sentiments which divide you from it'.") Ideas more suitable to men of wisdom than to artists, at least in this wonderland of today.

His show at the Palma Gallery in 1951 was a critical success, but pre-war enthusiasm for his work was lacking. The pictures were well painted and the subjects chosen — houses, still lifes, boats, people at the market — were treated with a simplicity that set off the abstract forms. The color had that typical value the artist uses naturally

PLATE 10

Paesaggio romano, 1956

to enhance his subject. What was lacking for these works to be masterpieces? Greater devotion to his task perhaps, a greater conviction of his own worth, a defiant attitude towards other people and himself.

It was with real pleasure, therefore, that I hailed the turn Mafai's art had taken in the past few years amid doubts and uncertainties but that has already yielded not only some masterpieces but also the creation of a new style. *San Lorenzo*, in the De Luca Collection, Rome, (Plate 7) gives an idea of the extreme point of imaginative freedom which Mafai had reached by 1945; a species of chromatic expressionism which did not prevent him from giving definition to houses, churches, trees. In *Veduta romana*,

PLATE 11

Mercato, 1956 De Luca Collection, Rome

1956, at the Tartaruga Gallery, Rome, (Plate 8) there is only a vibration of color, that is to say, the life of the objects without the objects themselves. The grandeur of a city without the city, all carried beyond reality and into the realm of poetry.

Perhaps the culminating work among these cities created by painting color, and poetry rather than by reality, is the *Paesaggio romano*, 1956 (Plate 10). It is perhaps the most abstract, although it gives a complete sense of reality.

Thus, because he had wearied of the way he had been painting up to that time, Mafai, without realizing it, and with his usual absent-minded audacity, solved on his own and in his own particular way the problem of the abstract and the concrete. And there is nothing sketchy about his new style; nothing could be more orderly nor

PLATE 12

Fascio d'erbe, 1957 Campilli Collection, Rome

reach a more logical conclusion; nothing could better represent pictorial effects, his love of Roman colors, his love for Rome itself.

The markets were a subject that gave Mafai the idea to use the sheets of canvas stretched like awnings over the various stalls for decorative effects, sometimes more and sometimes less accentuated. In his *Mercato*, 1956 (Plate 11), the awnings are whitish, but they serve as resting points in the general effect of spatial depth which is attained through quick touches of red and orange on a background of greenish violet.

Mafai's pictures of flowers have given fine results; he has been able to give free rein to his imaginative sense of color. In his *Fiori*, 1957 in the Franchetti Collection, Rome (Plate 9), he gives hardly any sense of the reality of the flowers themselves.

The entire stress is on the relationships of the greens and the reds and the purple background. The culminating painting of this series is *Fascio d'erbe*, 1957 (Plate 12), where formal precision is lacking but where, on the other hand, the vitality of nature is intensified in the contrast between the yellow and green mass placed against a background of two different shades of purple.

Mafai's new style, a species of liberation for the painter, was adopted by him in 1956 with the precise aim of obtaining a harmony between his work and social conditions of today. He tries to denigrate his own worth through a superlative conscientiousness and prefers to point out its negative aspects. He has written, for instance, "Man is no longer the center of today's reality. He is neither the protagonist nor even one of the actors; the actors are other things. In this exasperated search for a mechanical happiness, in this process of automation, man as an entity becomes ever more negligible... Faced with such dehumanization, painting tries to adjust itself to the new reality and places great importance on the form and the material, avoiding the problem of content... The character of the artist no longer corresponds to the usual concept; he has nothing in common with the Modiglianis, the Van Goghs, the Scipiones, with their charm and their human imagination. The artist of today organizes his instincts and filters them through his cold and astute intelligence, that is to say by making use of those qualities which are peculiar to our times." [5]

Were Mafai a critic it would be easy to start arguing with him and make him realize that his desertion of the portrait form does not mean that he has given up the humanity of man. If this were the case architecture, in the thousands of years of its existence, would never have been a human art because it does not represent human images. On the contrary, man today knows how to give vent to his energies even through the use of matter which he believed to be dead, and he dominates the world as never before and is able to display his imagination with just a few touches of color. But it would be wrong to argue with Mafai because he is a painter rather than a writer. In order to know his art properly it is important to understand his romantic return to a past that he believes gone forever, to the heroes of paintings towards whom he seems to turn with a feeling halfway between despair and resignation.

A painter from the time he was born, Mafai appears today to be an artist in spite of himself. But let us not complain; this is a proof of his sincerity, of his spontaneity, of his creative ability. He has experienced the most dangerous theories as a species of test and has come through them unharmed, thanks to his creative imagination which is invulnerable.

[5] *Il Punto*, October 5, 1957.

RENATO BIROLLI

I remember the impression Birolli made on me when he came to see me in Paris; he was a good-looking, smiling young man, optimistic for no particular reason but rather on account of a spontaneous active inner force, so continuously optimistic that he was not even aware of this feeling. We talked about Cézanne and Van Gogh, and his conversation did not betray that he had just arrived from Milan and was by no means my contemporary. And he told me how European artistic culture was developing in Milan, more or less under cover, in spite of Fascism and the domination of the Novecento school. That visit of Birolli's came to mind when I was in Milan shortly after the Liberation and found he was having a one-man show at the Santa Radegonda Gallery, where artists and poets met and looked forward to the future with that same faith that Birolli had kept firm even during the difficult years. When I visited him in his studio in the summer of 1954, I saw his paintings ready to be sent to New York, he still had the same smile and the optimistic outlook. In the meantime Birolli had become a painter of international repute and the favorite artist of the Cavellini Collection, Brescia, which is so valuable to our knowledge of contemporary Italian, French, and German art. There is no secret, psychological basis for his optimism. His art suffices to show us the final results of his inward energy rather than its source.

Birolli, the son of a baker, was born in Verona in 1906 and completed a course of study at the Institute of Technology and afterwards attended life classes under Guido

PLATE 13   *Bocca di Magra*, 1952 Cavellini Collection, Brescia

Trentini at the Cignaroli Academy. He moved to Brescia in 1928, where he easily obtained his diploma as a teacher of drawing. His first independent work, a painting of San Zeno, was inspired by the romanesque statue in the church of San Zeno in Verona; it was Birolli's hail and farewell to his native city and its patron saint before he became a

Milanese by adoption. This work dates from the end of 1930 when the Novecento style was predominant.

And yet Birolli's *San Zeno* already shows his preference for a techinique entirely dependent on color consonant with the ideas and the moral precepts of Edoardo Persico and with the painting of the "Sei" in Turin and of Scipione and Mafai in Rome; this reliance on color was contrary to the official Novecento school style. *San Zeno* shows a light and delicate color sensibility, a rejection of monumental plastic form and a devotion to Matisse, who has been Birolli's favorite master in spite of the various experiments he made.

Birolli was therefore completely ready to join the budding Milanese revolt that in 1937, under the name of "Vita Giovanile" or "Corrente di Vita Giovanile", was the forerunner of the better known "Corrente".

He painted portraits of his mother and father in 1932. The latter has the finer color, a light yellow jacket and pink flesh tones on a gray background. Although his painting at this time was superficial, he had already developed an individual style.

Naturally, as soon as Birolli succeeded in one direction, he tried a different one; in 1934 he began his Eldorado series of paintings, all of which had the same subject and served as a basis for research; the paintings in this series have points in common and points of difference; their form of Expressionism is easy and untroubled. Two years later he painted *Il Caos*, where the forms disintegrate beneath the fury of his brushwork and the pure color: purple, yellow and black. His trip to Paris in November 1936, and his direct contact with the Impressionists enriched his palette, calmed his violence and gave him a lesson in painterly refinement. In *Ragazza*, 1938, there is a painterly quality he had never formerly attained.

Birolli was in prison for political reasons in Milan in 1937 and in Verona in 1938 and was one of the group prosecuted in what was referred to as the "Trial of the Milanese intellectuals."

At the outbreak of the war Birolli went into hiding at Cologno di Melegnano, near Milan, where he worked until 1943; in that year he painted *Ragazza col cappello*, where the expressionist influence is mature and strong.

In 1944, when Italy was a martyr to German wrath, some of Birolli's drawings were published in an underground newspaper. He did a number of others that he issued under the title *Italia 1944*, a Conchiglia publication, in 1952. These drawings show the horrors of the war of Liberation, the brutality of the executions, the wretchedness of its victims, but the interest the form arouses is so strong that even the most distressing of the drawings has an allure that goes beyond mere illustration.

Campo di grano and *Vigna morta*, 1942, are two works in the expressionist vein

PLATE 14   *Rovi e strada*, 1953 Cavellini Collection, Brescia

which I admired at the Santa Radegonda Gallery for their imaginative freedom of expression; they can be cited as being among the best Italian works of that period.

Le Cupole di San Marco, 1946, a painting magnificent in its color and its ability to give a Baroque movement to the Byzantine cupolas, shows Birolli's continuing in the expressionist vein which he exploits easily and with artistry. There is an unfulfilled desire to escape in this picture. The necessity to start all over again if one does not wish to overdo what has already been overdone, if one wants to join the European tradition, not through a process of thought, but directly and decisively.

In 1947 a group of young artists founded the *Nuova Secessione Italiana*, which later became the *Fronte nuovo delle Arti*; at the 1948 Venice Biennale this group had great success and made headway, although a few less convinced members dropped off on account of an article written by Togliatti in defense of Soviet Neo-realism. Birolli was one of the most decided to refuse of the whole group; he had spent the year 1947 in Paris and in Brittany (Trinité-sur-Mer), and he went back there in 1949. He had the great humility to start studying again like a twenty-year-old student. Naturally he was accused of imitating Picasso, and some of his "miners" echo that master. He had, in the meantime, become master of that both allusive and abstract form which had begun with Cubism fifty years ago, and which is still a vital language in painting.

Birolli felt that the form of post-Impressionism and Expressionism which he had employed up to that time did not give sufficient freedom to his imagination either where reality or where form and color were concerned. The formal structure of Cubism allowed him to modify reality according to his imagination's need and at the same time to find independent harmonies between form and color. The imaginative transformation of natural reality, however, does not imply an absolute preference for the abstract. The abstract can be regarded as an object transcending our world. But Birolli had his feet firmly on the ground of this world of ours and intended to give form to his imaginative sense of perception and feeling, to his vitality that is expressed in every line and in every shade; even though he integrated part of his formal designs and made them vibrate with his own reactions to reality. This style is called abstract-concrete or can be described as the application of intelligence to life. Because of his lively reaction to the world around him, Birolli appeared to be more of a realist than many of his fellow painters.

The lessons learned from Picasso were essential for learning the abstract-concrete language; but even later this smiling Veronese painter was more attracted to Matisse because he shrank from the catastrophic aspect of Picasso's energy, even though he had acquired the latter's formal articulation, whereas Matisse's dream world of color had a fatal attraction for him.

From 1948 onwards Birolli's painting had a personal quality, thus any resemblance to the forms of Picasso or Matisse was simply coincidence; but these two names,

PLATE 15

Incendio, 1956 Campilli Collection, Rome

Picasso and Matisse can be useful as symbols of Birolli's different mental attitudes. There is a rhythm in his production, the formal organization sometimes consists of precise lines and the use of color is simplified and restricted; at other times the color prevails, full of pleasing sensuality. Both types of paintings are necessary to the formation of the painter's creative rhythm. A useful comparison can be made between *Barconi a Trinité-*

sur-Mer, 1947, and *Le Cupole di San Marco* of the previous year. Each fishing boat is worked out in Cubist style, that is to say, an organic form has been invented to represent a fishing boat, a year before this would have been beyond Birolli's powers; he has repeated the fishing boat pattern a number of times using now more, now less color, space and light.

The subject of *Ragazza alla finestra* has also been repeated a number of times, always with the aim of finding better organic form. *Case a Parigi* also dates from 1947 and is a typical example of how abstract forms can give a realistic effect. In 1949 his use of color increases and acquires its full intensity by allowing the greens and light blues to occupy rather large areas. *Tavola*, for instance, is a free composition where form and color are blended to perfection.

Later Birolli's style developed steadily along one line. He traveled a great deal; in 1952 he toured the Gothic cathedrals of France and Germany; in 1953 he traveled in Spain. During the summer he worked in different places: at Fossa Sejore (between Fano and Pesaro) in 1950, 1953 and 1954; in 1951 in Portobuso on the Grado lagoon; at Bocca di Magra on the border of Liguria in 1952. From 1949 onwards Birolli stopped worrying about changing the direction of his work. He was a master of his own style and painted with full confidence in himself.

Pesca atlantica, 1950, exhibited at the Biennale of that year, is a happy composition. It is a typical example of this painter's formal organization. There are many references to reality. He has even included his own self-portrait, as well as fish, nets, and piles of ropes. But the form of these various subjects is given by a happy, dancing rhythm. The sea exerts a great attraction on painters who wish to increase their use of color. At Fossa Sejore, Birolli not only saw the surface of the sea but also its reflections, and he worked out his painting *Sopra e sotto il mare* on the basis of light blue and green zones. In 1941, at Portobuso, he concentrated on greater integration of subject and background, as in *Molo adriatico* and *Scarico del pesce*, for instance.

Bocca di Magra, 1952 (Plate 13) shows renewed interest in the greater use of color, which is richer than before because the articulated pattern gives it support. *Rovi e strada*, 1953 (Plate 14) has a brown and green pattern on a gray and green background where his imagination freely creates a garden unsubstantial and never seen before and yet completely true as a product of the imagination. It is a typical case of imaginative strength creating a vision, an artistic reality that parallels the material one and is just as real. *Periferia milanese*, also of 1953, shows flowers in dark blues and violet tones interwoven in the foreground against a light background of yellow and green.

Cataluña de fuego, 1953, came out of his travels in Spain and shows the severity of formal construction applied to reality perfectly recreated, that almost seems realistic although it is not. Birolli produced a lot of paintings at Fossa Sejore in 1954. They are his best things up to that date, both for the richness of color and the severity in handling the subjects. *La laguna è bianca* is a masterpiece of closed pattern, full of movement, where the concentrated vitality of the boat contrasts with the diffused light on the water. *Ora forte meridiana* is a finely organized painting which harmonizes surface with depth and gives a sensation of the weight of noontide without illustrating it.

The urge to create patterns was one of Birolli's characteristics; another was his way of casting himself adrift on a color harmony where pattern is a mere pretext. In Birolli's painting, the pattern dominates and contains the color harmony. This benefits the final painting when the fusion between form and color is absolute. In *Bocca di Magra*, for instance, the fusion is complete but the colors are quiet tones of brown, green and pink. Since 1955 Birolli, instead, has freed his colors, as if a chromatic explosion had occurred in his work through which color is steeped in light and reaches the limit of intensity.

A visit to Cinque Terre in 1956 gave Birolli the idea for a series of paintings on the themes of harvest and fires. In one of the latter in the Campilli Collection, Rome, (Plate 15) the fire becomes an explosion and the pattern, identifying itself with the fire, takes its energy from the immediate fusion of light and color without any definite contours. It is an expression of that vital energy which sums up Birolli's personality.

In 1957 he spent five months in Antwerp; he worked a great deal in that city; the cordial welcome he was given warmed his heart, and he was carried away by the fullness of the Flemish sense of life, happiness, and energy. *Canto popolare fiammingo* (Plate 16) has a pattern defined by high and low vocal passages and with color contrasts that give a comic note to the scene. Birolli himself commented on this series; "I did a certain number of paintings in the theme *Canti Popolari*. The value here is on the sound, high and low, male or female, sad or happy, I could not express it through visual forms. Following an instinctive idea, I used certain forms as a base, some were half moons; others resembled tongues of flame; I used them in different positions, separately, in groups, I turned them up or down or sideways in close or scattered order. The color plays a great part in expressing the type, the quality and the value of sound. For this reason I did not think of the people who sang but of what the sound did. I may even have chosen a particular place as a complement to the expressive intensity. *Canto a margine di palude* is an example of one of the paintings I worked out in this way. I sold one of these series in Belgium and the buyer of his own accord immediately renamed it *Quatorze Juillet*, because he felt it had the optimism and the directness of certain popular anthems.

PLATE 16

Canto popolare fiammingo, 1957 Viviano Collection, New York

"It is my belief that I have overcome the last remaining obstacle (a dualistic conception of the world) to the fusion of objectivity and subjectivity and that I am directing my work towards its proper goal."

The attempt to represent sound through form and color is an old quest. In Italy

PLATE 17   *Incendio d'alberi*, 1957 Viviano Collection, New York

it was loudly proclaimed by the Futurists. Birolli has taken it up again today with greater refinement and with a subtlety which restricts but at the same time concentrates his forces. Half-moon and flame-like shapes, in groups or arrayed against each other, are found in the same effusion of color which has lost its fiery quality and become light and violet toned. It brings to mind a recollection of sound with that tinge of melancholy common to all memories, rather than the sound itself. Birolli's daring, his constant youthfulness, are held in check for a moment of meditation that does not diminish his sprightly imagination, but refines it and makes it more intimate.

In most of the work he produced in Antwerp the pattern is completely absorbed by the general pictorial effect. The artist, realizing this, called three of his paintings *Espansione* (*Effusions*) because the color mass expands and spreads over the entire painting. *Uomo nella landa* is a magnificent harmony of light and dark tones. In *Incendio d'alberi* (Plate 17) intense red is used for the effusion of color and in the broken forms that in itself expresses creative energy and without any further reference to reality. The abstract quality of *Alla ricerca*, 1956, (Plate 18) is, if anything, even more complete.

A moral problem is naturally linked to a change of vision such as took place in recent years and more particularly with an awareness of his work that Birolli himself has attempted to explain: "Inspiration, as I understand it, is an unlimited number of impulses that come to me mainly from what I see but also from an extension of the act of seeing to the imaginations as a whole.

"First of all I collect these impulses on my canvas and then I look at them, and here is where my work begins. At this point I feel the visual reality dissolve into another element which can scarcely be compared to the former.

"I eliminate some of the elements, double or treble others, until they coincide with what I wish to express. In this way a quantitative amount of impulses first becomes an expression of quality and hence of color and of form.

"I believe, not in optic space, but in the continual wave motion of that phenomenon, which never grips a probable object with its teeth or never inspirers dead or solitary forms.

"This is the only space in which I feel myself a man without preconceived ideas and continually reborn. And it is for this reason that centripetal elements are continually arrayed against centrifugal ones in my work.

"My imagination, whether working inside of me or outside, which procedure, however, is semi-automatic, enriches the first determining impulses. For this reason the concept of reality is more a mental process than an instinctive one. I can get in touch with nature today not through my interest in a fragment (such as a view through a window), or on account of the weight of matter, but as a way of perpetuating a vital adventure of its phenomena of transformation."

54

PLATE 18   *Alla ricerca*, 1956 De Luca Collection, Rome

In Italian contemporary painting Birolli stands out as a strong and daring spirit who
undertook the difficulties of art like a fearless crusader, and, although keeping in touch
with the greatest artists of today, followed his own line, concentrated on his own research,
happy and confident in his own strength, which represented the continual triumph of
his own imagination.

The complexity of the task he had set himself shows his daring. He did not wish to cast tradition aside. In fact he stressed the need for pattern, even if he then transformed tradition and pattern until they became unrecognizable. His imagination therefore was fairly free, but it was built up of reality, allusion and indications; and it acquired exceptional force as a theoretical argument continuously defeated by his creative energy.

It is atrocious to think that anything one says now about Birolli must be referred to the past. On May 3rd this same year he died suddenly. It is difficult for his friends to believe that his youth, his energy, his optimism, his marvelous creative spirit **are no more.**

SANTOMASO

GIUSEPPE SANTOMASO

The first time that I returned to Venice after the war I was delighted to discover Santomaso, an artist who had already found a personal solution to international pictorial problems. The works he showed me then are not those I like best today, but I recognize that he would not have reached the degree of maturity he has today without the experiments he made then.

Three years later, at the first post-war Venice Biennale, the critics were surprised to find a host of new Italian painters, unknown until that time and daring and confident, worthy of membership in a world avant-garde. Herbert Read expressed his own surprise concerning Santomaso, who "rises above the crowd to make an individual contribution to contemporary art." Rejecting the pedantic classifications of *abstract* or *non-representative*, Read considers that Santomaso "shows in his work his immediate and sensitive response to his surroundings," and catches the vibration of Venetian light in order to transfer it directly to his canvas without "the artificial devices of intellectual perception. He remains in the ambiguous world of feeling where forms and colors seek their equilibrium and their image." The art of Santomaso "has overcome the limits of so-called realistic painting and succeeds in arousing a sense of the duration of time, of continuity, which is the basic quality in sensation."

I have quoted these lines of Herbert Read's not only on account of his authority

PLATE 19

Ottobrata a Marino, 1955

as a critic but because he touches on an essential point for the understanding of this artist — the emphasis he puts on sensation.

Before examining Santomaso from the critical standpoint, it should be noted that in 1953 and 1954 he won more prizes than any of his fellow artists; besides the prizes given him at Trieste and São Paulo, he won the first prize at the XXVII Venice Biennale and was recently awarded the Marzotto Prize.

Santomaso has mastered his particular brand of the international style and carries it out by expressing his sensations without losing himself in intellectual artifices; and he pleases everybody, he pleases the critics, he pleases the public, more in fact than do his fellow artists. This means that the clarity of his expression overcomes in some way these conditions set by modern taste to which the public is generally hostile but which he succeeds in fulfilling.

If one looks for a reason for this affinity between his sensitivity of expression and the public's pleased acceptance of it, it can be found in the enchantment of his color. Santomaso's sense of color is too easily explained by saying that he is a Venetian. It is preferable to recognize his sensual temperament that he sublimates through contemplation.

I have an exact recollection of his room at the 1954 Biennale. The works dated from various years, 1941 to 1954, and the quality varied; the subjects differed too, they were derived, some to a greater and some to a lesser degree, from real objects; but there was a constant rhythm of color. In *Il muro del pescatore* the relationship between the brown and gray pattern and the sky-blue background was amazing on account of the energy of reality, dark and close at hand, and the far-off imaginative quality of the blue. I realized then that even plain shapes, large and dark, were a spiritual interpretation of reality close at hand, and that the light backgrounds, blue, green, or yellow, with their quality of infinite distance, expressed the sweetness of dreams. All contemplation of the lagoons, all attempts to escape from sensual reality, all memories of dreams about to vanish, are expressed in these light-toned, far-off backgrounds. This is the quality of Santomaso's color and this is his poetical expression.

Giuseppe — Bepi to his friends — was born in Venice, September 26, 1907, and studied at the local academy of fine arts; he first showed at the Ca' Pesaro Gallery. The earliest artistic circles he frequented were those of Gino Rossi and Pio Semeghini. He was invited to Amsterdam in 1937 and exhibited there; Van Gogh's paintings made a great impression on him. During his return trip, he was greatly taken by the paintings of Braque, Matisse, and Bonnard, but not by Picasso, which were on show at a large exhibition in Paris. Of Braque's paintings he preferred above all those painted in the 'twenties, that is to say, those least influenced by Cubism. It was much later than Santomaso understood the advantages of Cubist construction. At that time he only had eyes for color values. This is where Braque's composition and color inspired

PLATE 20

Laguna, 1956 Borgenicht Gallery, New York

him, whereas in Matisse he enjoyed the pattern since that painter was less interested in structure.

Santomaso's work up to 1942 was the result of his contact with these styles. He concentrated on still lifes, such as the three pine cones of 1951. The decorative intent is obvious and this is stressed by the superficial arabesque along primitive Baroque lines with a juxtaposition of patterns arranged at random in a time sequence rather than handled spatially. The artistic quality derives from the color, which is somewhat luxurious and occasionally attains real beauty.

Other still lifes of this period that have the same feeling include *Melograno e merletto*, 1939, in the Della Ragione Collection, Genoa, and other works of 1941, *Natura morta con bucranio*, Jesi Collection, Milan, *Composizione* a rather successful painting, and *Tre Sedie*, in the Cairola Collection, Milan. In 1942 he painted *Figura*, now in the National Gallery of Modern Art, Rome, which shows the influence of Symbolism rather than of Matisse and where a certain severity of composition can be noted without any relief or volume.

In *Composizione, brocca rovesciata*, 1943, in the Zannini Collection, Trieste, one sees that Santomaso has takes a new direction. The composition is no longer on the surface but in depth. The objects are arranged transversely and their volume is stressed through a contrast of light and dark tones. The constructive rather than the decorative feeling is dominant, not because of any new experience but because of an inner necessity.

This departure is, in fact, a cautious approach to Cubism, a sort of pre-Cubism, based on Cézanne, where he concentrates his efforts on the pictorial quality. *Sedie e stufa*, in the Pomaro Collection, Schio, *Brocca di Peltro*, in the Boldi Collection, Trieste, *Mandola e Tappeto viola*, in the Asta Collection, Venice, and *Stufa pentagonale*, in the Arnolfo Marchiori Collection, Venice, all painted in 1943, follow the same trend.

In 1944 Santomaso was in hiding from the Germans and concentrated on drawing rather than painting; he illustrated Paul Eluard's *Grand Air* with twenty-seven drawings, some of them linear and others pictorial.

In 1945 he worked on the human form. *Suonatore ambulante* and *Testa di donna*, in the Meneghelli Collection, Johannesburg, are among his best productions of that year. The artist is already a master of his own style, the structure is integrated and not added to the image, and is carried out in full by means of the color values. *Donna con gli agli*, in the Biondi Collection, Alessandria, and *Donna che dorme*, in the Hansburdt Collection, Trieste, as well as some other small nudes, all dating from 1945, are examples of this particular phase. These images have an expressionistic character and their aim is to reveal the anguish of that period. This is a direction that could be followed indefinitely, but is perhaps unsuited to Santomaso's temperament, to his placid nature, or to his need for contemplation.

In 1946 he seems to draw too close to reality and be unable to avoid over-objectivity. The *Fronte Nuovo delle Arti* started this same year however, and Santomaso felt he must put realism and expressionism aside and concentrate his attention on the architectural values of his pictures and so modify natural objects that, although the form given

PLATE 21   *Calda notte di vendemmia a Castelfranco,* 1957 Morton D. May Collection, St. Louis

them is based on theory, they will express the products of the imagination rather than reality. This is the abstract-concrete manner adopted by Santomaso in 1947 and which he has adhered to ever since. It has enabled him to achieve color harmonies that he hears inwardly and to absorb spiritually all that he sees around him.

His *Finestre* are an invention dating from 1946; he looks out on to the world, peering at real objects but only seeing those of his dreams. For this reason windows have become the symbol of his art, the theme common to all his works, such as *Finestra*, 1948, in the Cavellini Collection, Brescia. The same subject can be found again in *Interno con cancello*, 1948, in *Il confine della palude*, 1953, in the Museum of Modern Art, Helsinki, and in *Muro del pescatore*, 1954. Giuseppe Marchiori, in his charming little book, *La Casa sull'argine*, 1954, tells of an episode of Santomaso's life among the country folk in a far-off village of the Polesine, where he succeded in opening the eyes of the inhabitants of this primitive community to the beauty as well as to the usefulness of their farming implements.

For Santomaso everything is a good subject for painting, the Grand Canal or the banks of the Adige, and the more deeply and poignantly the subject affects him, the better his paintings are.

I could mention *Finestra*, 1947, in the Nino Festa Collection, Vicenza, *Finestra*, 1948, in the Gualino Collection, Rome; *La casa del pescatore*, 1951; *Officina*, 1951, at the Ente Turismo, Belluno; *Peschereccio*, 1951, in the Gallery of Modern Art, Turin; *Ritmi rurali*, 1952, in the Morlotti Collection, Milan; *Cantiere*, 1952, at the University of Trieste; *Finestra sulla Rotta*, 1952; *La Vite viola*, 1952, in the Cavellini Collection, Brescia; *Ritmi rurali*, 1954, in the Museum of Modern Art, Rome; and many others that are carried out to perfection. Santomaso comes to life invariably and completely in each one.

Many of these paintings are reproduced, some even in color, in Marchiori's monograph written in 1954. *Ottobrata a Marino*, 1955, is reproduced here (Plate 19). The richness of its color is even greater than in Santomaso's preceding works, and the sonority is fuller and more triumphant.

The award of the top Biennale prize has increased Santomaso's confidence in himself and made him more daring. In the works exhibited at the 1955-1956 Rome Quadriennale he already showed greater freedom of imagination, the subject becoming gradually more fused with the color composition. But Santomaso gave the finest proof of his achievements in his first one-man show in New York held at the Grace Borgenicht Gallery in 1957, a very successful exhibition. If some of his subjects after the *Finestra* sequence appeared arbitrary, this was the result of their incomplete fusion with the chromatic composi-

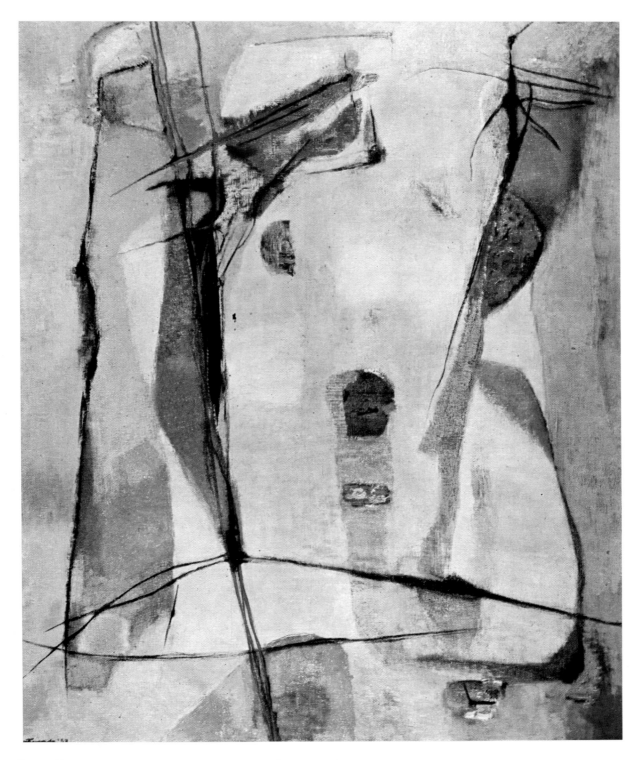

PLATE 22   *Sentimento della natura*, 1957 Paul La Rivière Collection, Montreal

PLATE 23
Ritmo verticale, 1957
Campilli Collection, Rome

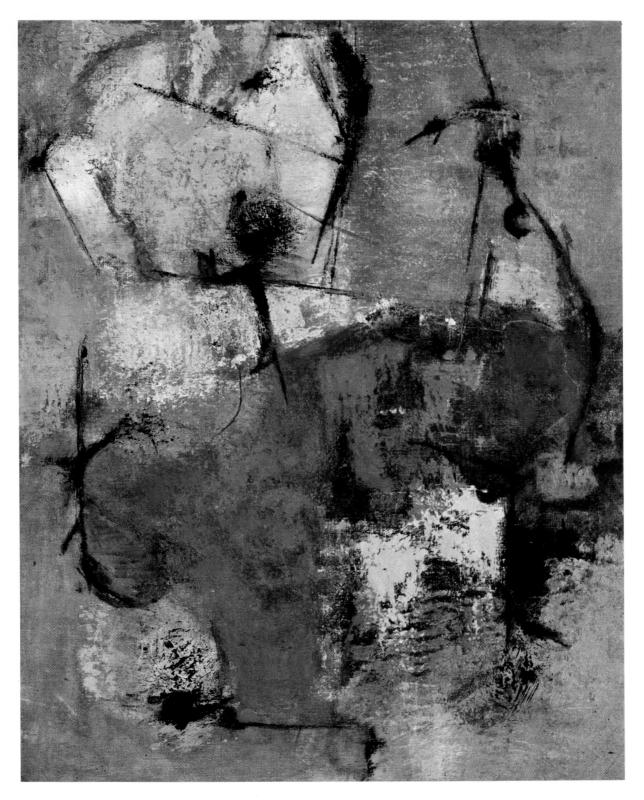

PLATE 24   *Carnevale assurdo*, 1958 Sambucci Collection, Rome

tion. The color itself was enchanting but the composition of the subject seemed merely an interruption that dispatched the color into a poetic distance.

Take a look at *Laguna*, 1956, Borgenicht Gallery, New York (Plate 20), at its wandering masses of black, pale blue, red, and gray, that seem to occupy various planes in depth. *Sentimento della natura*, 1957, in the Collection of Dr. Paul La Rivière, Montreal (Plate 22) is more nervous, dynamic, and restless; there are pale blue lines in the clear atmosphere and some harsh red touches. *Calda notta di vendemmia a Castelfranco*, 1957, in the Morton D. May Collection, St. Louis (Plate 21) is a brilliant singing red, a paean inpraise of heat, barely veiled in night blue. It is difficult to imagine a clearer or more determined reality, even though it is an imaginary reality, a recollection of the sensation of heat.

In all his recent paintings the color intensity that Santomaso reached in 1957 absorbs the subject. In *Autunno inquieto* there are masses of color without definite contours. *Basti in bleu* has a fine closed rhythm and several superposed planes, *Dalla parte della meridiana* is particularly charming, even formal, and sets the imagination winging towards mountains and threatening clouds. *Ritmo verticale*, 1957, in the Campilli Collection, Rome (Plate 23) is among his finest paintings; the reds and yellows float on a swaying background of neutral tones. The function of the pattern is to give an airy lightness to the colors. *Carnevale assurdo*, 1958, in the Sambucci Collection, Rome (Plate 24), shows the need for fusion between subject and background in order to achieve homogeneous art.

In an interview Santomaso gave to the United Press, May 24-25, 1957, he described his methods. When some particular nature object draws his attention he paints it as a spontaneous echo of the impression received without any interference from mental processes. The critical process starts after the painting is on canvas. He examines the different lines and the forms, some he keeps, others he alters, still others he rejects. In its corrected form the painting inspires him with new alterations and this continues until he is completely satisfied with the result. The work of correction and alteration comprises not only aesthetic evaluations but also recollections of his own life and of the ancient Venetian tradition.

Santomaso's strength lies in his feeling for nature and for color. He is not a theorist; he does not have the verbal subtleties of many of his fellow artists. But he leads a full and sensuous life that shows itself in his ability to transform the world into a dreamland of color. Full of recorded sensations and memories the color slowly drifts into the atmosphere. Romance for Santomaso means the contemplation of color; it is kept within bounds and determined by his need to be really convinced that his pictorial mastery is the sure basis of his dreams.

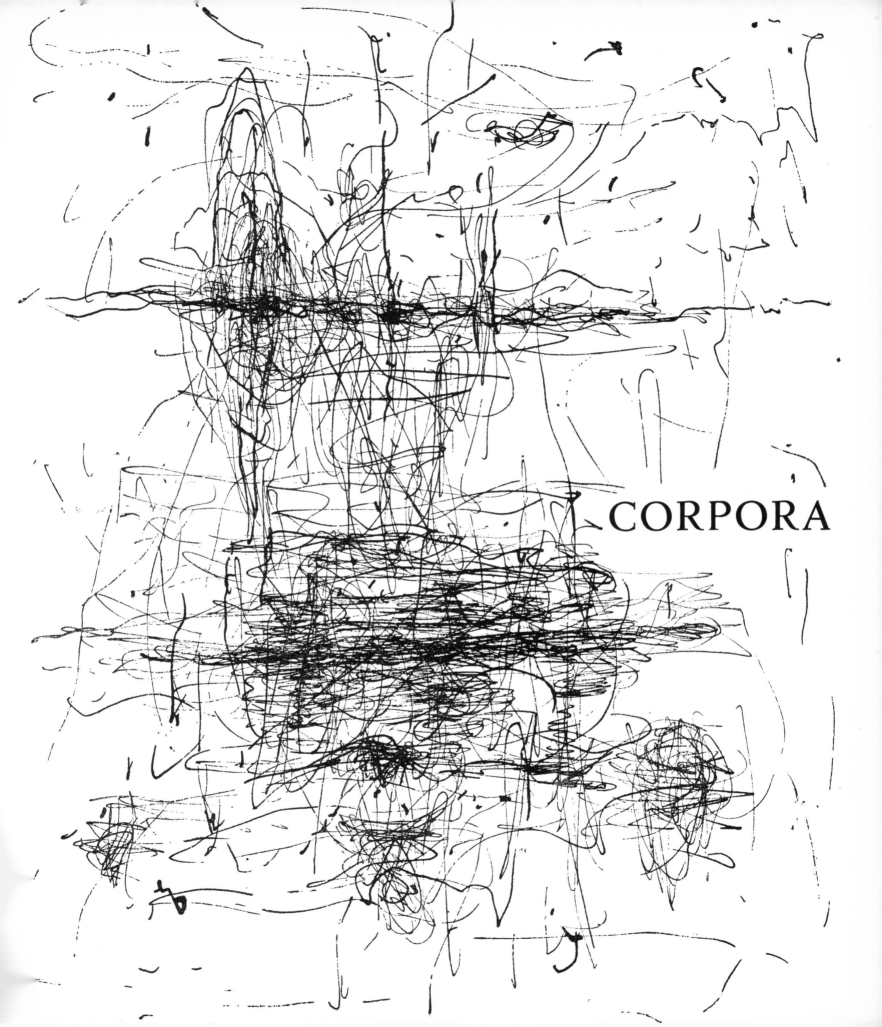

CORPORA

ANTONIO CORPORA

Some of Corpora's personal characteristics should be stressed, since they are part and parcel of his painting. He is above all a Sicilian, although he was born in Tunis in 1909, and he has the turbulence and the ingenuousness of his race. His long sojourn in Paris made him a greater master of the modern artistic tradition which developed in Paris than most other Italian artists and for this reason he has a definite idea of the gulf between academic and other art that precludes any possibility of compromise. Finally he has that combination of culture and intelligence necessary to the critical spirit by means of which he integrates his experience as a painter with his theoretical ideas.

On account of these characteristics Corpora drew public attention from the time of his first exhibitions in Tunis, 1928-30, and in Florence where he went to have an exhibition in 1930 and to study — that is to say to copy paintings hanging in the Uffizi. Aniceto del Massa declared in the *Illustrazione Toscana* of March, 1930, that he had faith in Corpora's temperament and in the results of his struggle against academism, which had enabled the young artist to work out his own moral attitude and to paint with absolute sincerity.

After Florence, Corpora went to Paris, where he found himself in the midst of the dominating French parallel to the Italian Novecento group, made up of painters like Oudot and Brianchon. But he also has leanings toward Matisse and Braque; he was less attracted by Picasso. It was natural that Corpora should waver at first between

PLATE 25   *Paesaggio*, 1954 Cavellini Collection, Brescia

the Fauves' and the Cubists' tradition and the more recent reaction. I have seen one
of his 1934 paintings — *Il Veliero* — where this crisis of indecision is obvious. But in
that same year his instinct led him to try Milan where he got into the Milione group
and met Carlo Belli. His pseudo-abstract period starts at this point, of which *Composizione*, 1937, is an example. Corpora showed this painting to Atanasio Soldati, who
told him that it was not abstract. It is, in fact, the representation of an imaginary

object. Moreover, at that time cubist tradition merely served Corpora as an exercise which he worked out diligently but without the enthusiasm painting needs.

The paintings in his one-man show at the Milione Gallery in 1939, after his fleeting experiments with other styles, had once more become figurative; it was favorably reviewed by Piovene in the *Corriere della Sera* of June 6, 1939, by Dino Bonardi in the *Sera*, June 13, 1939, and by Raffaele Carrieri in *Illustrazione Italiana*. I have seen two *Still lifes* of 1939, one of which is in the Luccichenti Collection, Rome. In these the form is created by color and is both vital and coherent. The colors are strong: yellow highlights and dark blue shadows. It is an expressionistic realism that stems from Van Gogh. His *Fiori* are delicate and appeal to the public. In this same year, 1939, Corpora returned to Rome; in *Villa Medici*, in the Natale Collection, Rome, he attempts to paint with the delicacy of Derain. Years later Renato Guttuso described Corpora's arrival in Rome [1]. "Even then he talked of 'quality', of unity of the matière, of 'language' and of severity; his formation as a painter and the style to which he adhered were clearly post-impressionistic, but a Post-Impressionism where stylization and construction intervened to modify the characteristics of this style as it was usually known and practised in Italy."

Corpora was again in Tunis when Italy entered the war. His painting was becoming more and more impressionistic. In *Fiori alla finestra*, 1942, in the Natale Collection, Rome, there are magic allusions in the size of the vase disproportionate to the landscape. *Paesaggio*, 1940, in the Occhipinti Collection, Rome, has a gentle color scheme, yellows and light greens against browns and light blues, but it represents a whirlwind that shakes the earth and carries it away; one sees in this painting the influence of Van Gogh and Soutine.

After the Liberation Corpora returned to Rome, where there was a fairly well established although restricted tradition of tonal painting, together with gropings towards exasperated Expressionism in the Soutine manner, which, although enthusiastically hailed by some critics, proved to be a passing fancy.

At this point the line which stretched from Rome to Milan and Venice took a different turn; the new trend adopted at that time has still a lively following and, for at least some time to come, will wield considerable influence. Corpora played a big part in this change of direction through his work and through his writings for the *Fiera Letteraria*.

I will quote some passages from his *Lettera a Raffaele Castello*, September 4, 1947, and from his article *Caratteri essenziali della pittura moderna* (Essential characteristics

[1] Fronte Nuovo delle Arti, 1947, p. 18.

PLATE 26 *Rosso e blu*, 1956 De Luca Collection, Rome

PLATE 27   *Due momenti*, 1957 Skira Collection, Geneva

PLATE 28   *Don Chisciotte*, 1958 Sambucci Collection, Rome

of modern painting), October 23, 1947, which were not his first writings on this subject but are the most detailed ones.

"It takes great knowledge, great technical ability, to discover what one does not have to do and what is not worthwhile expressing. The dead part of our work consists of concepts tied to hieroglyphics that we often mistake for ideas. These concepts are the habits of our heart and mind, our routine from which only a genius can escape completely. This is why we used to believe that in order to be human we had to bind ourselves to living reality, to imitate the timeworn way of representing human figures or objects. True humanity does not consist in habitual sentimentality but in understanding; a person who *understands* has seen the light of truth, and an artist's goodness consists in his moving desire to communicate this to others.........The drama of war completely shook any belief in the possible survival of tradition and made the desire for security based on old concepts now outmoded appear absurd. People became aware of a new reality, of a new kind of beauty fit for our new civilization, so unlike that of the past, less intellectual but more alive, where man himself is the dominating problem in every mental process. Picasso and Matisse appeared as the forerunners of this process, they had shown the way. A nucleus of young painters, followers of these two masters, break away from the overworked naturalistic tradition, and seek to work with the humility of new primitives; an act of faith in a moral scheme of things that allows an artist to breathe easily, to have an easy mind concerning the work to be done, in a future that stretches to infinity. In this way improvization, fear, cynicism, and exasperation were all overcome."

"These young painters succeeded in directing cubist abstraction back to its classical goal; its forms and colors arranged according to a highly lucid and narrative system and, above all, a love for objects and man which illuminates the matière cleanly and clearly, this love being the greatest new element. This secret love, still timid towards things and beings will help art escape from its solitude: the painter once again speaks to mankind, and mankind without conscious knowledge or volition is taking the necessary steps to approach the painter."

"These young painters are bound to the two fundamental discoveries of modern painting: the transposition of color and volume in space. These were final discoveries of both the Fauves and the Cubists whereas they are the starting point for the young painters of today. The process might be the reverse of that employed by artists who started with Impressionism, went through various phases and arrived at Abstraction. It may be said that today, starting from Abstraction, they are going back to conquer symbols, a slow process. All the younger generation of painters has done so far is to select and sort out their means of expression, they are evolving a method for balancing color and volume transposition according to the requirements of representation."

At an exhibition held at the Galleria del Secolo in 1946, it was my fortune to grasp the importance of this movement, I wrote about it in *La Repubblica*, January 4, 1947, as follows: "Since the end of World War II some young artists who refuse to listen to the usual invitations of the return-to-nature school have found new realities through abstract or pseudo-abstract forms. There are many of these young artists in France, Belgium, Italy and England; in the United States they are legion. Recently the Roman public has been able to see some works of Monachesi, Guttuso, Turcato and Corpora, but luckily these artists are not the only ones. In Italy the problem is the same as elsewhere: to reach an agreement over a common language to which each one will add his own particular accent. The essential problem of style is the creation of a common pictorial language."

These Roman painters were called Neo-Cubists by such critics as Marco Valsecchi in *Oggi*, February, 1947, when they exhibited in Milan. In the meantime they got in touch with Birolli and Morlotti in Milan, with Santomaso, Pizzinato and Vedova in Venice and, together with some sculptors, prepared the first exhibition of the *Fronte Nuovo delle Arti*, which was held at the Galleria della Spiga from June 12 to July 21, 1947. Giuseppe Marchiori wrote a fine introduction. The *Fronte Nuovo's* big success came at the 1948 Biennale, where all its members were widely represented. Some of them dropped the pictorial ideal on which the *Fronte* was founded on account of an article written by Togliatti. Corpora naturally remained faithful to the principles which he had helped to establish through his international experience. He received various prizes from 1948 onwards; the most important of these was the Paris Prize, which he was awarded by a jury under the chairmanship of Jacques Villon. Later, in 1952, he had a one-man show in Paris and Christian Zervos wrote the foreword to the catalogue. Various critics, Christian Zervos, Pierre Francastel, André Chastel and Léon Degand recognized the outstanding worth of Corpora's painting. Christian Zervos' long monograph published in 1957 was preceded by one in Italian by Guido Ballo, for which I wrote an introduction. He is appreciated by a wide range of critics, not only by Giulio Carlo Argan and Nello Ponente but also by Virgilio Guzzi, who is anti-Abstraction; as a result Corpora has become famous both at home and internationally.

Corpora's painting up to 1945 belongs to his prehistory, that is to say to the world of experiments in many directions which precede the formation of a style. Some of these experiments take abstract form; others consist of passionate outpourings without any precise form. Anyone who can conjure up a blend of these two tendencies has a basis for understanding Corpora's style.

There are many forms geometrical and others, that overlap each other to form the image of the little ship, its volume, the contrast of its light and shadows, its weight and its disorder, that is the subject of his painting *Vaporetto di Capri*, 1948, in the Franco Venturi Collection, Turin. It is a real object, not the little boat we have seen plying its way to Capri but a ship evoked by the imagination and no less individual for that. It even seems to be an old vessel that has difficulty in making headway. This description is sufficient to show the sentimental attitude of the artist towards his image.

In *Marina*, 1947, the construction of space and intensity of light is particularly successful. Some figures still appear at that period, such as in *Ragazze del porto*, and this endangers the formal coherence. *Il Porto*, 1947-48, in the Scarpa Collection, is a work that suggests natural reality through the use of almost abstract forms particularly well. There is a third dimensional space which is not realized materially but very vividly imagined. The same may be said of *Cantiere*, 1948, in the Landi Collection, Rome.

In *Navi*, *porti*, *reti*, shipping, the port, and fishing nets appear and disappear in the artist's vision, and finally the onlooker reaches a strange condition in which he can no longer distinguish the real from the imaginary, which is without doubt a poetic achievement.

Composizione, 1950, in the Cavellini Collection, Brescia, is one of the most abstract of Corpora's works; but it is, however, easy to distinguish the movement, like a wind of passion, as well as the decorative intent. *Canarino, gabbia e finestra* in the Museum of Modern Art, Paris, is also abstract, but the space is more obvious and there is greater dramatic contrast in the movement.

It was in 1951 that the dramatic intensity of Corpora's composition increased. *Moby Dyck*, 1951 in the Zadok Collection, Milwaukee, the painting which won the Paris Prize, is an example of this powerful intensity, with the forms ejected into the foreground and lights rotating in space.

Corpora's dramatic effects are ingenuous; that is to say, they are neither forced nor rhetorical. Hence this series is interrupted every once in a while by quieter paintings where the representation of an imaginary reality in space is carried out with a naturalness which is both surprising and pleasant. Such as some of the 1952 paintings, for instance: *Il Vecchio porto* in the M.G. Collection, La Chaux des Fonds, Switzerland, *Cantiere*, in the Pellizzari Collection, Arzignano, *Rocce e mare* in the Cavellini Collection, Brescia, are some examples of these quieter paintings. But in 1953 a new dramatic quality becomes apparent in such works as *Porto d'Africa* in the De Luca, Collection, Rome, and in *Mediterraneo* in the Cavellini Collection, Brescia. *Mediterraneo* is typical in its contrast between subject and background. The colors are blue-black against greenish-white. The subject is dynamic and therefore creates space in depth, but that space is represented objectively rather than felt through the color itself.

PLATE 29   *Muro dell'Infanzia*, 1958 Pogliani Collection, Rome

In 1954 Corpora enriches his painting by using deeper colors and extending the total color area. Since 1948 he has become a master of color, of harmony without shades or without chiaroscuro, of the ability to use color for indicating a position in space or in depth. As his means of expression became more intense, his color harmonies developed harsher and more violent contrasts. But a new life has infused his color in recent times. There are fewer lines, in order to allow color-volume to dominate the composition. The basis of Corpora's color is dark blue and green, to which he adds touches of reds and yellows. These touches are absorbed by the blue and green, as though by a dramatic necessity, they amalgamate, not without a struggle, and a human cry appears to issue from them.

Paesaggio, 1954, in the Cavellini Collection, Brescia, (Plate 25), is a good example of the absorption of both composition and form by color, which gives unity of vision with subject and background no longer divided but uniting to form a single and very vital object. Thanks to this unity the subject is developed in depth and the requirements of its development fill the space without any need for the latter to be represented.

When Corpora's production had reached this level, it had become more happy and thoughtful, which can be seen by his following "confession."

"My sort of abstract painting has never been loyal to the rules, I have used intense light as a spatial dimension for a long time and this has often been interpreted as impressionistic light by academic theorists.

"Since 1944 I have used thicker matière and worked it more, not because I enjoy affectation, but simply because matière has a mysterious side of its own and a different importance to that given it by painters of former generations. A special world with its own light and its own struggles lies inside the few square inches of a picture, like the worlds in the universal kingdom, and although the matière exists and has density the painting nevertheless has infinite space. A painting as a universe is composed of these different worlds, self-contained and harmonized (even through their contrasts) in a thinking and pulsating nucleus.

"The language we use today for expressing ourselves is neither figurative nor abstract. It merely infers absolute freedom in the search for novel forms that can only be justified by the artistic emotion that has inspired them. A language, therefore, cannot be ahead of time because human reactions in space and time cannot be foreseen.

"An infinite number of painters who believed that they had found an easy means of expression through non-figurative art, a safe way of mass-producing mental sensations and emotions, one day found themselves treated as academic, whereas but yesterday they had been revolutionaries.

"The only possible historic process is the one that takes place within ourselves and by means of which a painter, who himself is the sum of his technical and human

80

PLATE 30   *L'Età della terra*, 1958 Galerie de France, Paris

experiences, starts afresh each time in order to arrive at the sum total of his learning
and his maturity of vision.   This is where they differ from the untaught anarchists who,
starting from scratch, with great audacity go straight to their final goal, caring for
nothing but the new discovery that is tantamount to a revelation.   For the latter in the
beginning, at the time the forms were invented, fine results were the only aim, but
almost immediately afterwards these painters were obliged to confine themselves to their

formula, as academic as any other, owing to a lack both of experience and of an overall historical viewpoint, the original aim being their sole and very restricted basis.

"Where I myself and my work are concerned, all I had at the beginning was an intuition and a general idea. My forms were nothing, formless blotches and lines, lumpy pigment, until through a revelation I discovered how to make something out of these blotches and lines that are the superstructure of a style, good workmanship combined with emotional overtones. Thus moderations bring order. Order and moderation and matière that belong to one work of art alone and that are revaluated in the creation of each new work.

"My 1957 works, in this sense, are freer and less severe than my former paintings because every last shred of security has been plucked from the emotion and the thought, every crutch of preconceived idea or sentiment. These paintings are more cruel, but only cruel towards their creator, but, on the other hand, full of feeling for man's destiny. In these works, which seem to me more inventive, less bound by rules but, at the same time better ordered and clearer, the light is never an adjunct but has the quality of volume, a vibrant body, and the area and weight of the dark masses equals that of the light ones.

"In closing, I would like to quote a phrase Pierre Francastel wrote about me: 'Corpora's work is not just a happy accident. It is a part of man's destiny...'. "

The expression 'man's destiny' can be understood when it is realized that emotion is always present in Corpora's work, that it dominates, unchallenged, in his recent paintings, that have been freed from the last links with representational art. A comparison of *Paesaggio*, 1954, with works such as *Rosso e Blu*, 1956, in the De Luca Collection, Rome, (Plate 26), or *Due momenti*, 1957, in the Skira Collection, Geneva, (Plate 27), emphasizes the change, the clarity of the individual components, the full-throated color, the vitality of the whole. I think the colored reproductions clearly illustrate Corpora's new expressive ardor. In *Paesaggio*, 1955, *Pomeriggio*, 1957, and *Mare del Sud*, 1957, the blacks have become more pictorial, that is to say more closely bound to the lighter tones with which they form patterns. The rhythm of *Pomeriggio* is a work of art in itself.

He gives great importance to the matière nowadays, or rather to the variety of the surfaces and to the resulting refraction of light. But he never introduces foreign objects into oil paintings because he is convinced he can obtain the desired effects with oil colors alone and doesn't want to take bargain short cuts. With him it is a question of conscientiousness, of control, of craftsmanlike severity. His attitude is that of a conscientious craftsman, controlled and severe with himself. And it is undeniable that the unity of painting style depends on the constant use of the same medium.

By 1957 his palette was almost monochrome, he was absorbed by the problem of the refraction of light and research always tends to become onesided. But as soon as he had mastered his light problem, his color exploded again, enriching to an incalculable degree the general effect.

Light and color therefore create an imaginary reality, as in *Don Chisciotte* (Plate 28), *Muro dell'Infanzia* (Plate 29) and *L'Età della terra* (Plate 30), all of which date from 1958. On the other hand, it is natural that these imaginary realities should be indescribable since, could they be given a precise name, they would lose their character of purely pictorial creations and become associated with natural reality. Corpora, therefore, does not represent things but the images of his desire, clouds that pass above the earth, poets' voices.

These paintings have no affinity with *art informel* because they display a constructive will: in *Muro dell'Infanzia*, for instance, the harmony between the various levels of surface and the spatial organization is highly accomplished. Thus Corpora's imagination is always controlled by the necessity of constructing a painting.

Imaginary realities, the variations of surface and light, the explosion of colors, the constructive control, the severity of his technique, are all various aspects of Corpora's art and of his aesthetic and moral strength. He is an artist who both thinks and dreams. He is now fifty years old, but one may be sure that he will not be satisfied to stop working and merely contemplate the results he has already obtained. He is a perpetually dissatisfied and passionate researcher; every year he finds something to say that he has not said before, and it is this passion of his that gives vibrancy and vitality to his ever-changing style.

AFRO

AFRO

Looking at Afro's paintings at the 1956 Biennale, I tried to forget that I knew him personally and sought to construct his portrait from the forms and lines of his paintings. Too often one starts with a man's personality in an attempt to understand him as an artist. The reverse process — to start with his painting and work towards his personality — is more valid because if the work is genuine, it contains the whole being of its creator.

Every work of his that I saw had its own individual characteristics, although there was a common stylistic affinity, not only in their composition but also in the form and color. I recognized a technique typical of a man who knows his craft or does his work with accuracy and enthusiasm. This, together with a natural elegance, engenders facility, something akin to a victory over the hard work required that the completion of the picture had entailed. A sincere sensuality becomes poetry through the delicacy of the sentiment expressed and shows the necessity of sticking to decorative elements even in moments of expressive intensity; this is a consequence of Afro's linking sensation to feeling. Then there is his attitude towards the world, his first approach seems timid but his attitude ultimately becomes decisive and courageous, so that he can allow himself to contemplate the world with the same freedom with which he has lived in it.

All this is not only part of his work but also part of the artist's nature, it is what makes his art valuable, it is the charm that can also be found in his private life.

It is obvious he has not always painted as he does now, but the development of his style has been gradual and follows its own internal logic in spite of the various inspirations that have come from the outside.

Afro was born in Udine, March 4, 1912, and finished his secondary education at the Venice Lyceum in 1931. He had his first show at the Milione Gallery in Milan in 1932. His father was a house painter. In 1936 Afro won a competition for decorating the Opera Nazionale Balilla College of Udine, a huge work carried out in the pseudo-primitive *Novecento* manner that was all the rage at that time, but Afro's work was not found sufficiently heroic or rhetorical and, in spite of the protests of the Italian Department of Fine Arts, it was covered with whitewash and nothing but a few photographs remains.

A year later, in 1937, he was given the job of decorating the Albergo delle Rose on the Island of Rhodes. In order to escape from the style he had previously used, he employed a modified Baroque

PLATE 31   *Balletto*, 1953 David Karr Collection, United States

PLATE 32

Pietra serena, 1957 Phyllis Lambert Collection, New York

style, an imitation of Venetian seventeenth and eighteenth century work. The result is an example of sparkling technique.

This past history has some bearing on his present style. On account of the confusion existing in critical ranks nowadays, his critics have even used these decorative qualities to detract from the value of his painting. If one opposes the terms decorative and constructive, one must agree that Afro has a very excellent and personal way of constructing his paintings. If one opposes the terms decorative and expressive, it appears to me that his expression is valid on account of the portrait of the man which emerges from his painting. I mean by this that Afro, in his best works he has painted between 1948 and the present, has reached a decorative, structural, and expressive unity. His way of bringing third-dimensional patterns to the surface is one of the most pleasing of this painter's qualities.

After 1937 his subjects were mainly still lifes that clearly show three successive stages in the development of Afro's style. One of these, painted in 1935, displays a

PLATE 33   *Stagione nell'ovest*, 1956 Viviano Collection, New York

number of objects cleverly arranged, well drawn, and with correct tonal values; it is the work of a young man who wants to prove his technical perfection to himself.

In another still life, 1941, in the Libera Collection, Roma, space is still treated in the traditional manner but the forms of the objects inserted in this space are extremely simplified and fewer in number. The effect of light dominates and absorbs the contours, giving painterly values to the objects and transporting reality into a distant dreamland.

By now the crisis was imminent. In *Natura morta con candela*, 1942, formerly in the Laudisa collection, Rome, the space is brought up to the surface, and the few objects painted with such sharp contrasts of light and shade and so simplified that they recall the Fauves, and hence are a foretaste of Abstraction.

The same thing happens to the portraits, some of which are painted in the impressionist style; *Liliana*, 1940, in the Libero de Libero Collection, Rome, is a particularly happy example. The form created through vibrant touches of color-light enables the imagination to express its spirituality without any sensation of the matière's weight. The same remarks apply to *Ritratto del Pittore Natili*, 1941, in the Lazzari Collection, Rome.

In another portrait, *Ritratto del Pittore Turcato*, 1942, in the Zorzi Collection, Trento, the simplification of the form shows that Afro's style is already headed towards Post-Impressionism. In *Ritratto di Maria*, 1944, his preoccupation with abstract geometrical form is obvious. A line from the face continues into the arm and forms an architectural spiral, even though the face is given character. But the color disappears because of Afro's preoccupation with form.

At this point some uncertainties can be felt in his style. *Ritratto di giovane con cappello*, 1944, in the Elsie Rieti Collection, New York, displays accentuated expressionist distortions. It is an extremely fine painting, although not in the artist's usual style. *Una donna che legge*, also of 1944, in the Romanelli Collection, Udine, is a variant of a Picasso subject, interpreted in flat areas of color. Two other still lifes of the same year show a couple of tables covered with a number of objects. One of these is in the Venice Gallery of Modern Art and the other is in the Attilio Crespi Collection, Rome. These paintings already display a perfect harmony between the abstract and the concrete and a need for formal architecture that does not hinder realistic representation. The influence of Braque is clearly felt.

Afro was working with the Resistance in Venice when the war came to an end, and this event precipitated the interior crisis which had been brewing for some time within the artist's mind. Its effect was to halt his artistic production. We know of two still lifes of 1947 where real objects are still represented, but in such a way that they dissolve into abstractions. Shyness drains his colors, they become pale, almost

PLATE 34   *Cera persa*, 1957 Smith Collection, Washington, D.C.

pastel-like. *Ritratto di Adriana Pincherle*, 1946, in the De Luca Collection, Rome, through the extreme mildness of the way he interprets the abstract, gives an effect of concrete life.

Pesci, 1947, in the Libero de Libero Collection, Rome, is a little masterpiece. There is a bewitching relationship between the yellow-green background and the light blue-violet-green tones of the table.

Afro's production in 1946 and 1947, however, is negligible; his development was

91

all internal; his talent was ripening. The fruits of this maturity can be seen in 1948, a year of intense activity. Afro had at last found his true bent and was making up for lost time. He kept away from the *Fronte Nuovo delle Arti*, and did not exhibit at the Venice Biennale, but he sent pictures to New York while waiting to have his first one-man show there. The discoveries he made in 1948 formed his personal style, the one which is best suited to his nature and evolves the way life does, developing but not changing direction. His form is abstract and his subject is presented rather than represented. This does not prevent his forms from having vitality and movement, and they find their *raison d'être* in this response to life. Space is not represented but exists through the part it plays in producing the image. At times one could say that space creates the image, at others that it is created by the image.

When Afro feels an emotion he does not represent it immediately but awaits its return; sometimes this occurs after a considerable lapse of time, and if it does not return it means that it is better to forget it. But when it does return, it takes on the color of legend and can be transmuted into painting. Afro doesn't make notes from life but from memory, and his drawings narrate emotions that surge up out of the past. In 1950 he spent eight months in the United States, but he did not paint any American scenes on the spot. He only painted them much later, when memory brought them back; the earlier emotion filled his spirit once again but in a way far different to that immediately experienced. His vision needs the intervention of time that favors the transition from the humdrum to the poetic. Perhaps this is why Afro's work does not consist of sudden improvisations, of rapid and brilliant intuitions, of proud conquests. Because he needs to project the subject of his imagination into the distance, his creation develops slowly but with the quality of having reached a definite goal. He has absolute faith in Abstraction's capacity for expression. With the attitude of a man who can do nothing to prevent the inevitable, he accepts its perils. This language is necessary to him because it is the only one which reveals to him the secrets of the soul.

In the work Afro produced in 1948 there is greater clarity and decision and also more consistency in showing the subject than in his earlier work. The new harmony of form is the result of his certainty concerning the relative importance to be given to the material object and to the symbol. One of his temperas, *Lis fuarpis* (The Scissors), consists in a harmony of static and dynamic forms carried out in dark and light tones, both on the surface and in depth; the brush-work is perfect. *Un padrone di più*, in a private New York collection, is an architectural abstraction that displays the same creative irony as a portrait of the *Ubu Roi* type. *Composizione*, in the Jucker Collection, Milan, stresses the forces and complexity of work which is human although given the semblance of a machine. *Occhio di vetro* and *Macchina*, in the Grosso Collection, Turin, are more fantastic; the pattern rears in space and both through its height and its particular allusions suggests magical meanings. *Dispetto*, in the Detroit Institute of Arts, is a tale of struggle and of resistance, a childish game, dangerous for adults.

Afro not only changes the nature of his subjects in 1948, but his color also acquires an expressive autonomy. Critics have noted that Afro uses colors one on top of the other like glazes, thus enriching his effects. This is a traditional Venetian way of using color, but Afro substitutes layers of glazes with juxtaposed planes where individual colors harmonize with the whole. In this way he obtains both clear individual colors and complex blends.

Afro reached a kind of perfection in 1948, but the following year new demands arose. In 1948 Afro had felt the need for isolating the motifs in some way in order to construct them and make them more expressive. But immediately afterwards he felt the need to express motifs and background simultaneously. *Paesaggio*, 1949, in the Augusto Caraceni Collection, Rome, represents an imaginary city that develops in depth without any distance between subject and background. A drawing of the same year, *La Vergine Savia*, in the Catherine Viviano Collection, New York, shows dynamic lines drawn with a Picasso-like frenzy. The harmony he found in 1948 disappears and, apart from a pause in 1950, Afro's style from 1951 until today has been more dynamic than in his earlier work.

In *Il Negro che taglia l'erba*, 1951, there is a strong image in spite of the articulated movement of the body and the whirling of the scythe. Those who know Afro's language see in this painting an obvious representation of reality in spite of the abstract forms used. The color in this painting is severe but not autonomous. It embraces the form in order to define the planes.

He did many landscapes in 1951 and used different aspects of natural objects as a pretext for depicting human emotions. *Scilla*, in the Calini Collection, Rome, is the rock that cannot be rounded; *Paesaggio destinato a Franz Kafka*, in the Ralph Lamberson Collection, New Haven, is naturally an obsessive game, and *Caccia subacquea* in the same collection shows a dramatic struggle between unknown monsters.

A certain relaxation which can be observed in 1952 produces freer and more complex pictorial values. *Rodeo* is an ironical painting based on the corrida; the bull entering the arena has the head of a fly. *Paura nel buio* is a child's obsession with incomprehensible shadows. The color is the basis of Afro's expression in this painting — the black producing an effect of fear; the child, represented by reds and whites, yearns towards the background, which consists of superimposed pink glazes. *Autobiografia* is a loving struggle of colors, pinks and whites against browns and greens. *Cow-boy*, in the Lee A. Ault Collection, New Canaan, has a fleeting quality, like the wind. *Villa Fleurent*, in the Venice Gallery of Modern Art, shows the painterly disorder of summer homes.

The development of Afro's 1951 style into that of 1952 and 1953 is important. Paintings of 1951 and 1952, *Paesaggio a New York*, *Canto Fermo*, and *Falso Barone*, all in the Cavellini Collection, show how well the artist can express a subject, which remains isolated, however, because it does not melt into the general color scheme. In 1953, instead, in *Cronaca nera* and *La persiana*, also in the Cavellini Collection, the color is vibrant and the motif is no longer distinguishable from the color as a whole.

In *Sigillo rosso*, 1953, Afro recounts one of his childish pranks. *Portico d'Ottavia* expresses the emotion for ancient marble seen by moonlight. The impression is one of enchantment, of bewilderment, and sadness. In *Pietra serena* everything is white and green including the reflections of the water. *Ottomana* is a stormy fantasy.

He displays only one tendency in the years 1952, 1953, and 1954. Among his finest pictures of that period are *Paesaggio con la luna*, where there is a dark blue pattern on a green and white background that is worked out in depth; the color of this painting is enchanting. *Balletto*, in the David Karr Collection, (Plate 31) was shown at the Biennale. The blues are truly a song from the soul, and there is human color in *Incontro* and *Figura distesa*, also shown at the Biennale.

In recent years Afro has gained a still greater and wider reputation which can no longer be denied, in spite of those critics who are, as usual, blind to his merits. The 1955 show at the Viviano Gallery in New York was very successful, and in 1956 the international jury at the Biennale gave him the first prize; the majority of the Italian delegates, alas, were not in favor of this award. It is a classic example of a man never being a prophet in his own country. That is a great pity where the taste of Afro's compatriots is concerned, but the honor conferred on Afro is all the greater.

By now it is patent that the technical perfection that everyone recognizes in his painting is the result of his having clarified his ideas, a process that consists in expressing theoretically all the vague impulses that arise from the subconscious. As Maurizio Calvesi has explained, Afro is not a surrealist, but he adopts surrealist elements and then masters them in a stringent synthesis. This accounts for the fascinating combination of dreamlike qualities with sureness of his painting and also explains his richness of feeling and the perfection of his technique.

In 1955 he wrote the following commentary for the Museum of Modern Art in New York:

"I often think of myself as a painter who is a story-teller. Were it possible to sum up in a line, or in the luminous quality of a color, my deepest feelings, my memories, my opinions, my intolerances, my mistakes and fears, the mysterious flow of my entire being could spill over into my painting voluntarily, so that the origin of all images

PLATE 35

La Candelora, 1957 Jaffe Collection, Los Angeles

would be found to stem from my personal life. For this reason I do not avoid such words as dream, emotion, lyrical feeling, that are nowadays rejected by those who want contemporary painting to express intellectual clarity and awareness of the methods used for producing certain effects." [1]

[1] *The New Decade*, The Museum of Modern Art, New York, 1955.

This state of mind, which Afro has described so well, is illustrated by his paintings of 1955 and 1956. Those of 1955 which should be mentioned include *La caccia subacquea* in the Carnegie Institute, Pittsburgh, *Estate nell'orto* and *Barocco romano* — an imaginary reconstruction of Baroque architecture — *Per una ricorrenza*, in the Pulitzer Collection, St. Louis; *Ragazzo col tacchino* in the Mrs. Stanley Seeger Collection, Texas — a cheerful and impudent monster. *Silver dollar club*, in the Jesi Collection, Milan — a clever rhythm of light and dark shadows — *Ombra bruciata*, in the National Gallery of Modern Art, Rome, *Stagione nell'ovest*, in the Catherine Viviano Collection, New York (Plate 33) — a successful and dynamic painting — and *Progetto di viaggio*, in the Herbert Mayer Collection, New York — a well balanced composition — all belong to 1956.

Afro has developed a new awareness; he now says: "I have worked very slowly in the last months, but in a way that seemed useful to me for sorting out my ideas on painting.

"For some time past I had felt uncomfortable about my painting. What I did was no longer the result of a process of evolution or the answer to an increasingly urgent and definite feeling of inner necessity. My painting had always been subjective. I have always sought to base my paintings on past events recollected through feeling and intuition; but recently certain representative symbols that formerly seemed to give order to my work, to establish a certain connection with reality, had lost their interest for me and came between me and the picture, preventing new discoveries. Certain figurative elements which I had formerly believed were necessary to me, although pruned to the point of becoming ideographs, now seemed depressing trash, as familiar as ciphers, but lacking the ring of truth. I felt far away from my work because I was no longer satisfied with the representation of reality based on imagination, on dreams, or on memory which had an existence beyond the picture, and of which the painting reflected or interpreted; I now wanted that reality to be one with the painting, and I wanted the painting to become the actual reality of the feeling, not merely a representation of it.

"I had allowed the pictorial image to form itself in an unexpected fashion, letting a form expand in a threatening manner, a color become too bright, the matière arise out of its own strata of calculation or *laisser-aller*. The blur of memory remains, a slow wave that engulfs all the flavor of a season, but no longer its outward shape, nor even the shadow of a shadow, only the infinite origin of remembered forms, rather than the limited although indefinite final revolt.

"Painting becomes its own inspiration, the life of feeling, the will power of the intelligence, a moral and imaginary individuality. The picture does not make allusions, but imposes its own being, secret and unforgettable, like everything one has dreamed to have or regretted losing.

PLATE 36

L'uccello del tuono, 1957 Stanley Seeger, Jr. Collection, Dallas

"Today I can no longer think of an artist — nor have I ever thought in this way — as a clown or as a magician who performs tricks. I see him rather as a plant that grows spontaneously in its natural element, blending the individual stature of his existence in the light of the whole."

Of his 1957 paintings, which Afro considers display his new strength and his new joy in painting because they are the result of his freeing himself of allusions, as he himself explained in the passage quoted above, three are reproduced here — *Pietra serena*, *Cera persa*, and *La Candelora* (Plates 32, 34, and 35). In spite of their differences in size they are a trilogy from the standpoint of color. In all three the matière is almost transparent and shows to what a pitch of refinement Afro had brought his technique.

In *Pietra serena* the tone ranges from white to a near black, with black used on the left as a starting point for the dynamic development of the picture. Its delicacy consists in its refusal to make any definite statements — everything has a fleeting quality, although the pattern is clear. Everything is gray, although an infinite number of colors are suggested; the sensation it gives is of a moment of breathless contemplation.

Cera persa has a yellow background, not just the color yellow but an expression of nature. It suggests an analogy with some sunset tints that seem human even though they are natural phenomena. Afro's yellow has a human richness and melancholy. The pattern, in white, blue and black, seems to take flight from this yellow background which enhances the light, clean look of the pattern's colors.

Gray, pink, and yellow are the colors which, in turn, accent these three paintings, which reveal three different spiritual stages.

La Candelora is intense in color, although it preserves a feeling of delicacy. The range is pink, of varying intensity, sometimes tending towards orange, sometimes towards violet, and broken by various tones of black. It is color without light or shade, but it gives a dream-like atmosphere.

Afro's dynamic qualities increase continually. In *Segno limite* there are a flock of colors, blacks, yellows, and grayed pinks on an almost white background. The touch of brilliant red and yellow make the whole vision vibrate. *Controforma* shows, with an irony derived from Goya, an imaginary white monster issuing from gray clouds. In *Tempera magra* the matière seems dry and gives the optical illusion of fresco. It is very colorful, although the colors used are few —gray, white, and black.

L'uccello del tuono, 1957, in the Stanley Seeger Collection, Texas, (Plate 36) is a synthesis of the various styles described above, with the expressiveness emphasized.

In 1958 I saw the decoration that Afro had painted especially for the new UNESCO building in Paris. It is a poem of shading, a potential rather than an actual creation in color, a work carried out in a gentle and reserved way, a testimony of a long civilization.

Afro's artistic nature reveals its splendor in his relaxed attitude, in the calm, deliberate way he works towards perfection, in his deep awareness of his own working methods which he now uses in conjunction with the natural facility that is one of his richest gifts.

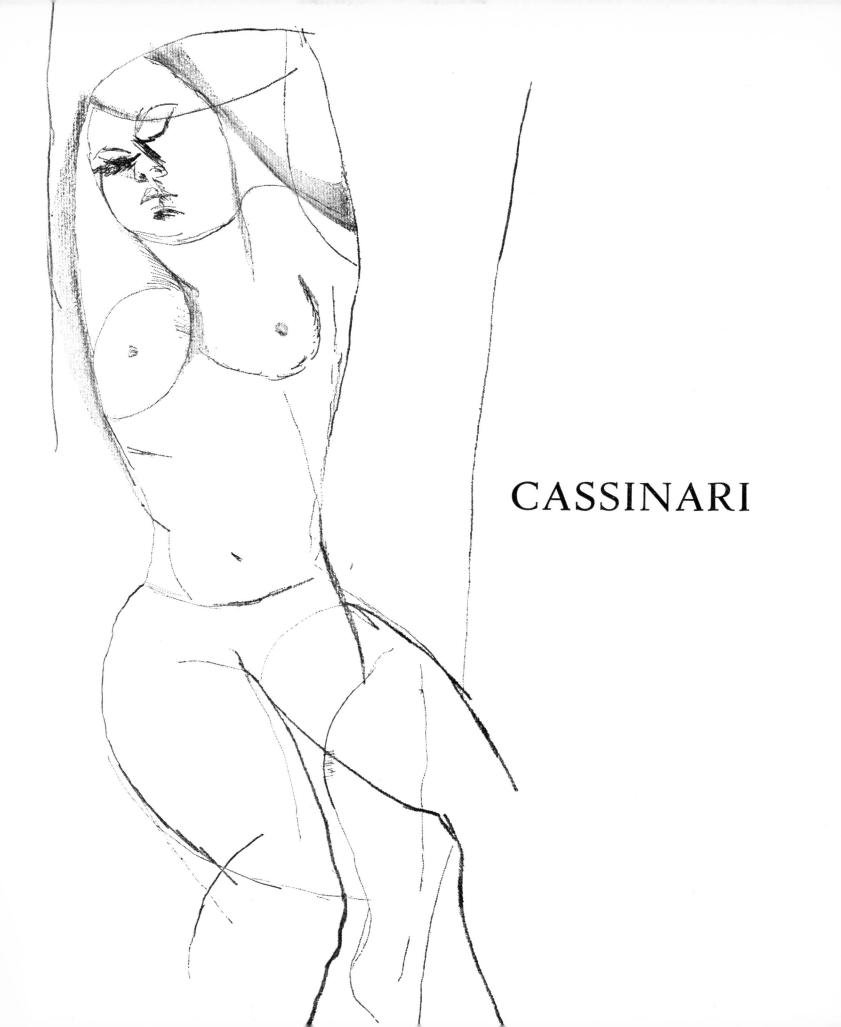

CASSINARI

BRUNO CASSINARI

My immediate impression when I met Cassinari was that he was pleasant but at the same time detached. He does not seek success, and he enjoys it from a human standpoint, even though success is not his goal. He doesn't take sides, whether it be for a political party or an artistic tendency. He knows that an artist can only assume responsibility for doing his own job properly. No one can challenge his craftsmanship; he is a dedicated perfectionist, and this is the basis for his sure touch. On the other hand he is not interested in accepting or formulating theories. Reality or abstraction, plastic form or colors are not theories for him but arise out of his work. His intuition may unconsciously produce results that display a clear and distinct theory. A similar creative process takes place in many other artists who do not claim to belong to the avant-garde. One might say that Cassinari belongs to the avant-garde in spite of himself. This is one of the reasons why critics comment favorably on his work. They have the bad habit of drawing him over to their side, some of them with the war-cry of "reality reality" and the others "style style," just as if the reality that Cassinari creates was not his own particular style.

Some of his plain but also profound statements clarify this point:

"I believe, now as always, that a canvas can only be painted through hard, up-hill, and difficult work.

PLATE 37   *Ritratto della madre*, 1955 Jesi Collection, Milan

"Something well done — that is what painting should mean, the sum of many complex tasks, values, and experience.

"For this reason every good painting of every period has the same ingredients. That is why quality creates a bond between paintings of all periods.

"The only true law is that arising from deep and exclusive dedication to work. This is why I am not over-enthusiastic about words or artistic manifestoes. Love of painting excludes any possibility of artifice, confusion, or even illusion. A well painted picture is an act of understanding and of will, and for this reason is also a good deed.

"I used to rely on my instinct, in which I had great faith. I believed that a painting was bound to emerge if, during its various stages, a selective process was used with care and ideas were allowed to mature. I now have less faith in the inevitability of this comfortable solution, and I try to *see* the image of the form with the greatest possible clarity before tackling the canvas. I have come to believe, more and more, that the splendor of the color should be determined through clear mental processes. For this reason I have a great admiration for Bazaine, "the layman," and Manessier, "the mystic," among French contemporary painters. In my opinion, the French school of painting, that is to say modern tradition since Cézanne, the style, the feeling for a painterly language, and even the apprenticeship system, are impeccable and far more rigorous than elsewhere. This school still sets an example for all of us today.

"My painting can never become abstract in the sense that it can become detached from the reality of sensations nor separated from the joyousness and presence of things. I have too much belief in the color of the sea, beside whose shores I am working for many months, I have too much belief in the splendor of the leaves, in the warmth of faces, I feel their weight too much to be able to prevent them from dominating my work. I feel that these presences require ever greater illumination. I continually attempt to give clearer expression to their weight through *rhythm*, and their warmth through *light*." [1]

There is no room in Cassinari's head either for abstract or for neo-realistic painting; all that interests him is that the painting of today should be part of painting through the ages. He sees his form clearly before putting it down; he sees it but he does not work it out. This was Cézanne's way; this is how those impeccable stylists, Bazaine and Manessier, work day by day in their studios. Cassinari feels the presence of the thing itself and creates the form of what he feels; this is the secret of his painting. His participation in the contemporary way of feeling form, his search for craftsmanship in execution, his matière, his contacts with painting of all time, make it possible for him to be simultaneously in the fray and beyond it. His form is vital, because it is full of perception and feeling, and it is theoretical because his awareness is not hampered by any set rules. Some of his outstanding characteristics are due to this essential condition.

Perhaps he is best known as the only artist of his generation that has created a type. He has painted his mother many times. He idolized her for her strong and energetic character. The mother type is continually present in his thoughts. When he paints a girl, he shows her youth and sometimes even her beauty, but this derives from the moral attitude emanating from the aspect of his mother. Nor is that sufficient; in a

[1] My thanks to Toti Scialoja, who collected these remarks of Cassinari for my benefit.

PLATE 38   *La Gravette* (Antibes), 1950 Campilli Collection, Rome

still life, 1952, in the National Gallery of Modern Art, Rome, even the objects take
on a maternal aspect from the moral standpoint. Cassinari knows that this is the way
it is, but I do not know if he is aware that this is the abstract aspect of his art.

An artist seldom reaches abstract form in order to give a moral value to things he loves and venerates. By means of a dramatic trauma he rises from the image of the thing to its type, from the matière of his painting to the idea of his life. This drama is responsible for the high quality of his art.

Bruno Cassinari was born in Piacenza on October 29, 1912. His father was a workman, but his mother succeeded in setting up a furniture shop. At the end of five years of schooling, Bruno was sent as an apprentice to a jeweler. There was a movie theater opposite his place of work with portraits of the stars, huge sunken eyes in pale faces, which the lad copied. His first love was sculpture, and at the age of twelve he modeled his first portrait of his mother. He was then sent to the Gazzola art school in Piacenza, to become an engraver of jewelry. At seventeen he went to the Umanitaria School in Milan, where he studied with Bogliardi and discovered the value of a great humanitarian tradition independent of the church's teachings.

He displayed his exceptional capacity for work in the years 1929 to 1933; he worked eight hours a day with his engraving in the laboratory of the jewelers and then went on to the Brera evening school for life classes. After supper he studied sculpture at the Castello school. He was admitted to the Brera Academy of Fine Arts in 1934. He followed their courses and painted a portrait of his mother. Besides what his mother gave him, he earned his living during the years he was at the Academy by engraving and modeling dummies for clothing stores. In 1938 he left the Brera.

A year later he won the first Littoriali painting prize with a neo-primitive composition. He held his first one-man show at the Corrente Gallery in 1940, and Elio Vittorini wrote an introduction to the catalogue; it was the first step towards future fame. This is what Vittorini wrote about him at that time:

"I am not taking sides in the argument over the Corrente Gallery, and I don't wish to connect myself with it; I do not deny any of yesterday's values, nor the day before yesterday's. On the contrary I still recall them as valid today; but I do not believe that painting stopped after Morandi, Carrà, De Chirico, Rosai, and De Pisis, but that it continued and that new painters are coming to the fore. The intellectual side has taken a strong hold, and this is just why I think that some people refuse to see a new trend anywhere. They have become used to myths and perhaps want other myths before they find anything acceptable. Why should this be? Mythology is not the only religion. There is also Buen Amor, and today, it seems to me that the future of painting lies in mysticism, in Buen Amor.

"Cassinari is an extreme example of mystical dedication. It is in his blood, together with the need to develop, to search, perhaps even to sweat blood in order to draw a cry of pain from the world by delving into its depths. No young painter of our times

PLATE 39   *Figura*, 1957 Pogliani Collection, Rome

has ever been so firm, right from the start, in his determination to obtain an effect of depth through the use of color alone. No painter has ever been so whole-hearted from the beginning, so successful in carrying out the task he set himself. Cassinari's recent landscapes are works already fit to take their place in the history of Italian contemporary art. They are neither tentative nor experimental. A blessing seems to have penetrated his hands."

Cassinari won the Bergamo Prize in 1941 with a still life. After the Liberation he won the Matteotti Prize and worked on a magazine, "*Il 1945*", edited by Raffaele De Grada, which combined advanced political views and avant-garde artistic opinions. In 1946 he joined the *Nuova Secessione*, but he soon became aware of the latent conventionality masquerading under an apparently new form, of the boring rhetorical slogans, with the result that when the *Fronte Nuovo delle Arti* was founded, he set off on his own. He held a second one-man show at Ghiringhelli's Galleria del Milione in Milan. He was at last able to visit Paris in 1947, and after his third one-man show at the Milione Gallery, 1949, he settled in Antibes and spent a great deal of time there until 1952. He held a one-man show at the Antibes Museum in 1950.

Success came to Cassinari without his seeking it: 1951 — he had a one-man show in Copenhagen and won the prize in Taranto; 1952 — the first international prize *ex aequo* at the Venice Biennale; 1953 — a special room at the São Paulo Biennale; 1954-1955 — an invitation from the Paris Salon de Mai and an award at Golfo di La Spezia.

Ever since 1931, when he painted a female nude and another portrait of a young woman inspired by Segantini's picture *Due Madri*, Cassinari wanted to produce fully finished work, "museum paintings." But when he was working at the Brera he discovered Modigliani through reproductions and so had his first revelation concerning the nature of contemporary art.

The atmosphere of the Corrente Gallery, financed by Ernesto Treccani, strengthened his opinion that it was necessary to rebel against the rhetorical mannerisms of the Novecento, "That painting famed for its virile and wholesome qualities." Fascism closed the intellectual frontiers, and this both spurred artists to rebellion and at the same time deprived the rebels of their necessary weapons. The name "Van Gogh," and an acquaintanceship with his work through reproductions hardly sufficed (in 1940!) to make one feel a part of European artistic life. Van Gogh was, however, the rallying point for the young artists of the Corrente group. According to Cassinari, only two masters had a "deep and liberating influence on his work" as a result of direct contact with their pictures. One of these, around 1947, was Modigliani, and the other Picasso, around 1950.

He definitely benefited from these influences, but it should be stressed that Cassinari's personality is so closed and detached that his assimilation of other painters' patterns has been very slow; as a result the international experiments perfected but did not radically change his art.

The self-portrait, 1933, in Cassinari's own collection, is academic in style but shows energetic approach. But *Portrait of His Mother*, 1936, also in his own collection, is already a work that deserves praise for its drastic simplification, its sense of form obtained without chiaroscuro and for the tonal effect of the skirt, black with red reflections, against a grayish-brown background.

Expressionism in general and Van Gogh in particular attracted Cassinari by their spontaneous leaning towards the simplification of forms, just as they drew his fellow members of the Corrente group and particularly Birolli. *Pietà* 1942, is an expressionistic interpretation of a subject-pattern that dates back to Gothic sculpture.

There is a *Natura morta* of 1942 in the Jesi Collection, Milan, which is low and reticent in tone. The white of the pitcher is lively, full of allusive vibrations, but the painting still lacks formal meaning. After this date a period ensued where Cassinari sought to determine his form, to give the effect of volume, to obtain an image built up in an architectural manner.

Nudo nella cattedrale, 1947, in the Andrea Caprotti Collection, Milan, is a typical example of Cassinari's work at this point. He forms his shapes through the use of color rather than chiaroscuro, and the incisive lines — Cassinari's famous wounds — provide the image with anatomy, although it may not be the anatomy of reality. The influence of Modigliani is plain in this painting. *Ritratto di giovane ragazza*, 1948, in the Pia Fiocchi Locatelli Collection, Lecco, shows that Cassinari had been able to carry out his aims effectively. The space surrounding the seated, immobile image of a motionless woman, shown as a goddess in her niche awaiting adoration, is divided into areas derived from Cubism. Modigliani has freed Cassinari from the bondage of true-to-nature proportions, and the contours of the zones and the incisive lines therefore become natural through the transcendental character of the image.

A year earlier he had painted a portrait of Beniamino Joppolo, now in the Jesi Collection, Milan, where one sees the combination of portrait characterization and abstract shapes that has now become an essential part of Cassinari's painting. His color sense is still dormant and did not awaken until a year later. *Il priore*, 1948, is a masterpiece. The formal shapes match the color mass and, taking on exceptional vitality, show the introspective character of the subject, while the red and violet tones make a singing contrast against the gray-blue of the background. Except for *Il cardinale*, painted in 1954-1955, this is Cassinari's best portrait.

In 1946 and 1947 the artist also painted landscapes that show his usual solid

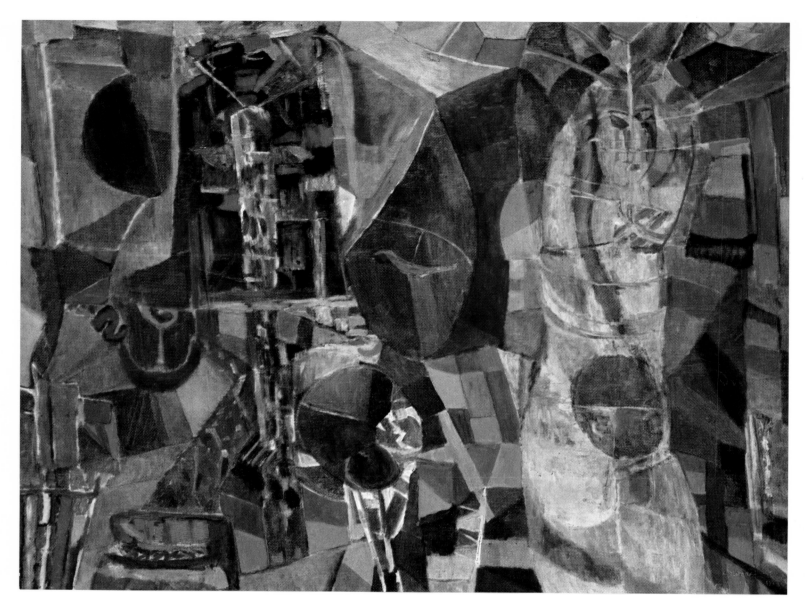

PLATE 40 *L'Atelier con modella*, 1956 Campilli Collection, Rome

construction but with a new feeling for color. Alongside of those warm colors that Cassinari considers "gallery tone," there are cold colors adopted from the impressionists.

The crisis came in 1948. It was then that he acquired an awareness of formal abstract values as a means of interpreting impressions of reality. This crisis took him to Antibes, where he practiced a more sweeping type of synthesis.

PLATE 41   *Festa al mare*, 1956 De Luca Collection, Rome

La buona pesca, 1950, in the Schettini Collection, Milan, shows some of the results
of this crisis. Everything is topsy-turvy, new light effects are hinted at, the images
are sketched in vaguely. In *I pescatori di Antibes*, painted in the same year, in the
Giuseppe Verzocchi Collection, Milan, similar results may be observed. The free handling of color outstrips formal delineation.

By 1951-1952 Cassinari had overcome this crisis; his solid intelligence had gained from all these experiences and from the discoveries he had made on the beach at Antibes of the liberties that could be taken with form and color. He had gained a less conventional and more lyrical approach that he was able to apply to his own tradition.

If one compares *Natura morta in rosa*, 1952, in the National Gallery of Modern Art, Rome, with his 1942 still lifes, Cassinari's achievements in that ten-year period are easily understood; it should be stressed that this is typical of the value international experience has for an artistic genius. In his 1952 work the light takes over its own areas, like the facets of a crystal; every object has a plane on which it can solidly rest in a well defined space that suggests a chronological sequence. Cassinari's complete mastery of the abstract style makes it possible for him to express everything around him, i.e., to give a concrete expression to the abstract. In *Lo studio*, also of 1952, in the Jesi Collection, Milan, one sees his nude model lying amongst his paintings, various heads, still lifes, and landscapes. It could be a realistic representation, but it is not because his sense of style leads him to put planes, spaces, and images in completely unreal or surrealistic juxtaposition, such as would be absurd outside of dreams. His colors, either used in sequence or in contrast with each other, harmonize in unexpected ways. Everything is orderly, although reason never limits his imagination.

The culmination of purely creative form, form without form, i. e., spirit freed from matter, has perhaps been reached in *Il Cardinale*, 1954-1955, in the Ettore Dell'Orto Collection, Milan. *Il Priore*, of 1948, is very fine, but it still displays some traces of the realistic tradition which disappear in *Il Cardinale*. The latter painting is conceived as an abstract architecture; it has a wraithlike quality, but also the reality of a lively human being more effectively evoked by an expression or a smile than by mere features. If one stops to think how much passion and enthusiasm are needed to create an image of this kind, one feels like singing the praises of such artistic miracles.

Cassinari painted many landscapes when he was at Gropparello, near Piacenza, and also at the sea. Landscape, for him, is a form of color composition that he carries out with unprecedented intensity and richness in a freely created arabesque. *Notturno marino*, 1954, in the Jesi Collection, Milan, *Pomeriggio al mare*, 1954-55, in the Dell'Orto Collection, Milan, *Estate a Gropparello*, 1953, *Ricordo della Sicilia*, 1954-55, are some of his finest landscapes. *La Gravette, Antibes*, 1950, in the Campilli Collection, Rome, (Plate 38) is represented here in order to convey, however inadequately, the intensity of Cassinari's color.

Ever since he painted the first portrait of his mother in 1936, in order to prove he knew how to paint, a new version of this subject has marked each successive stage of his development. He was already a master of Abstraction by 1952, but he juggled with that style to produce an image full of force, movement, and grandeur. It is a

110

PLATE 42   *Natura morta*, 1957 Sambucci Collection, Rome

monument to his feelings of admiration and devotion. In the 1955 portrait of his
mother, in the Jesi Collection, Milan, (Plate 37) he felt the urge to use explosive colors,
fiery reds and yellows. The moral grandeur of his mother is diminished, but there is
an increased feeling of joy, although mixed with anxiety, in this loving and fiery image.

111

This is perhaps the ultimate expression of Cassinari's filial reverence; anything further would be merely an exercise in painting.

Figura, 1957, in the Pogliani Collection, Rome, (Plate 39) clearly shows how Cassinari's brush deals with a female image when the moral significance of maternity is missing; there are separate areas of color like precious enamels that give the image a fantastic and fairy-like appearance.

Cassinari has not changed his style in recent years, but he has developed it further. *L'Atelier con modella*, 1956, in the Campilli Collection, Rome, (Plate 40) succeeds in absorbing the pink image of the model into the composition as a whole, through a juxtaposition of light and dark tones. *Festa al mare*, also of 1956, in the De Luca Collection, Rome, (Plate 41) is a stupendous color composition where references to real objects become increasingly vague and where there is an effect of fireworks and a night seascape. The sea is dark blue and the depth of this color carries the emotional content of the picture. *Natura morta*, 1957, (Plate 42) shows an easy organization of the color composition; plants bloom against a background red as a sunset.

In this period Cassinari spent a great deal of time in Paris, but he opposed the neo-impressionist tendencies of Bazaine and his group.

He continued to stress the construction of his shapes through geometrical patches, without too much emphasis on depth, following cubist principles. But his geometrical patches become progressively more abstract, making his painting more coherent. The abstract shapes touch one another with the object of strengthening and intensifying the fiery quality of the color. In this way Cassinari has simultaneously attained his goal and reached the perfection he has always sought.

TURCATO

GIULIO TURCATO

It is common knowledge that Turcato is a born painter, that he lives for painting, and that from his earliest youth he has done nothing but paint. In 1942-43 he taught drawing at a technical school in Portogruaro, and since 1953 he has been assistant professor of life drawing in the Rome artistic Lyceum. Besides this, somebody has always turned up to buy one of his paintings; this is how he makes his living. His official position and his reputation are greatly inferior to his work, partly because he is shy and not interested in any public recognition; in spite of his having been through some difficult times he is satisfied with his Bohemian life, the only one he considers worthy of an artist, because besides being free it is the symbol of freedom. But Turcato's form of anarchy is an extremely gentle one, Venetian in character, that would not harm a fly and so disinterested that it is a work of art in itself.

If to the above one adds that he can work very hard, although never steadily, and often with long intervals between one work period and another, one realizes that if he is not widely known, if even the value of his work varies, it is his own fault. Now is a good time to discuss his work, as he has been working intensively and successfully in the last two years, during which he has renewed himself.

Turcato's essential quality, which fellow artists such as Corpora have recognized, is his sense of moderation and the subsequent total absence of rhetoric. When Turcato turned to pure abstraction, for him it was neither an experiment nor a game, on account

114

PLATE 43 - *Le Mosche cinesi*, 1957

of the spontaneous integrity of his painting. It never even occurred to him to use a line or a color merely to show off rather than to express an emotion or suggest an idea or a poetical allusion. Turcato's strength lies in his insistence in expressing his own visual fantasy, which often makes him forego "picture-making". For this reason his paintings appear and often are incomplete, even though true creations from the standpoint of artistic values; just as in the past, few artists are able to escape the compulsion of completing a painting.

It seems to me that I have gathered here even too many reasons that explain how it is that Turcato's reputation is inferior to his true worth: shyness, indifference to public recognition, a Bohemian way of life, intermittent working habits, sense of moderation, delicacy, even tenuousness of inspiration. These are all shadows cast by the light that emanates from Turcato's true artistry.

He considers his art to be completely abstract and distinguishes three types of abstraction: the American, as represented by Pollock; the French; and the European, of which Hartung is his favorite artist. Poliakoff he considers too romantic, Matta too surrealistic, and Manessier too bound to Impressionism. Among Italian painters he likes Corpora, Vedova and Afro, of the younger painters, Dova and Perilli.

He is not interested in Mondrian's Constructionism, because, according to Turcato, a picture is a space filled with emotion, without center and without the doors of a triptych. He thinks that Surrealism has been useful because it has allowed thought to unfold freely, outside of any literary tradition. All he needs to start painting is to feel an emotion that can spring forth from the picture's boundaries and serve as a surrealist impulse without help from the subconscious, capable of being expressed in form and color without romantic drama. In his opinion painting creates space in perpetual motion, free of any theory and able to transform and modify the existence of feelings, which is always relative.

Giulio Turcato was born in Mantua, 1912, and has Venetian traits because he lived in Venice and studied there in his youth, until he finished his secondary education. He then attended the Academy, or rather the life classes, before he went to do his military service in Sicily in the years 1934 to 1936.

After he left Venice and went to live in Milan, Turcato went through a long period of crisis that he refers to as his "nomad period." He was in one hospital after another on account of illness and began to feel the need for a serious approach towards life and work and also to realize the relativity of results. "There are many different types of people in hospitals, and their reaction to death also differs. It differs, but on the whole it is fairly resigned. One can't do more than so much, one can only make wide generalizations that take different aspects according to the nature of the person."

The "nomad period" lasted a long time, from 1936 to 1940, but fortunately it was interrupted from time to time. It was at this period that Turcato made architectural drawings for Muzio, a Milan architect, and came into contact with the Corrente group, which he did not join. He himself explained in *Realismo*, March-April, 1955, that cultural redemption, the desire to make contacts with France and for moral renewal, as a reaction not only against Fascism but also against the entire preceding generation, had pre-

116

PLATE 44   *Scoppio di maschere*, 1957 Canali Collection, Rome

pared that need for redemption which produced the Resistance. Turcato had no patience either with cultural imperfection or with that childish romanticism he saw even in the best movements of the period, such as Corrente.

In 1940 he returned to Venice. He paid a brief visit to Rome in 1941 and a longer one in 1943, and it was during these visits that he became a Communist and joined the Resistance. In 1943 he exhibited for the first time in a group show at the Zodiaco Gallery, Rome. After the Liberation he painted landscapes in the Roman School style, influenced by Mafai, but soon he turned towards a sort of Neo-Cubism; this tendency is apparent in the work he exhibited in a joint show with Corpora at the Secolo Gallery, towards the end of 1946.

At that time Stradone, Scialoja, Sadun and other painters were against the neo-cubist group. It was the period at which the decision as to which style should be adopted was a problem that went beyond personalities. In 1947 Turcato felt he needed to go to Paris, and there he fell under the spell first of Magnelli's type of abstract

PLATE 45

Il deserto dei Tartari, 1957

art and then of Kandinsky's. On returning to Rome he took part in the *Forma 1* movement that held a show in Via Margutta, 1947, and later exhibited in the *Mostra d'arte astratta italiana* promoted by *Forma 1* at the Roma Gallery in 1948. In the April 1947 issue of *Forma 1* he published an article entitled "Crisi della pittura" (Crises in Painting). After discussing Cubism, the Fauves, and Picasso he wrote:

118

PLATE 46   *Composizione*, 1957

"What relationship is there between these movements and Italian painting? Such relationships have never been clearly defined; in our opinion, Italian painting was active on the fringe of these movements and has not yet succeeded in coming out of the blind alley. The misunderstanding arose from the belief that a language especially made to convey the meaning of another era could be modernized indefinitely. Modern expression consists instead in a new feeling that is subsequently expressed through completely new forms. Now the fallacy of Realism is being offered as a bait. But what Realism? The Realism created by Caravaggio in contrast to the mannerism of his times... This aesthetic theory hides the same fallacies as Carrà's primordial and primitive style, that is to say, through a false cultural finish, it tries to give new life to a form of panting that still echoes Italian nineteenth century art, to turn back the clock, when the rest of the world is searching for a new style that is still nonexistent. This fallacy has taken in even young Milanese painters who believed that they had accomplished their task when they had adapted a Picasso-like Expressionism to the romantic Lombard characteristics. The only remedy is to seek out a new kind of form, but naturally only the sort of man who is fully aware of what is going on in the world and is in contact with it can do this, the artist who sees a future stretching ahead of him and not the man who continually turns back on himself, on a formation riddled by sentimentality. This is why we consider the experiments of the first Abstract painters important, although we personally took a different stand."

I would like the reader to bear in mind that the lines quoted above were written in 1947, and that they have a prophetic value where the later evolution of Italian painting is concerned. Those painters that remained to the Novecento School, those who stuck to Realism or added a pinch of Lombard feeling to their imitations of Picasso, missed the boat. As early as 1947 Turcato understood the historical situation of painting in Italy better than many more eminent and apparently knowledgeable people. The problem is that, in order to understand the history of painting, one must understand painting, and Turcato is a born painter.

After exhibiting with the *Fronte Nuovo delle Arti* at the 1948 Venice Biennale Turcato found abstract art condemned by the Communist party, of which he was a member. This obstacle, which arose right in the middle of his natural line of development, did not leave him unmoved. In various ways, through representation of figures, through symbolism and even Surrealism, he tried to reconcile his convictions as a man and as an artist. His artistic nature prevailed, however, and he had sufficient anarchy in his character to disobey orders from his superiors. He even came to blows with Cagli and Guttuso in defense of his liberty. Turcato did not refuse to depict certain social themes, such as *Comizio, Rivolta, Rovine di Varsavia*, (Political Meeting, Revolt, Ruins of Warsaw),

PLATE 47

Arcipelago, 1958

but he represented them in abstract forms, a heresy since it destroyed their propaganda value.

In the meantime he won a fellowship that enabled him to make a long stay in Paris in 1950, and he has returned there many times since. He also traveled in Germany and even as far as China. Thus, in his own way, he dominates the international art horizon.

Composizione, 1947, is still neo-cubist, and he not only builds up the pattern but also the entire picture with space clearly defined. There is a certain static quality in the forms in spite of an attempt of dynamism in the contours.

Composizione, 1948, is already abstract, however, with a pattern independent of the background and hence of the picture as a whole. This picture is full of energy, but the movement is still forced. One can detect the influence of Magnelli in the stress given to sharp edges, although this influence is already in decline.

Composizione di rovine di guerra, 1949, belongs to another world, invented by Kandinsky, but where the floating quality of Turcato's imagination shows itself to perfection. The dark areas flee like undifferentiated and uninterrupted cries swept away by a storm to a far-off place in pursuit of their destiny. One must go back to *Guernica* to find a similar subject and to understand how Turcato succeeds in completely expressing his own vision, even with his light-hearted approach.

Composizione, 1954, already has the rich colors that distinguish his most recent work and which make it possible to establish a link between even sharply defined areas. This is the first example of his use of webs, a reticulate pattern used by the painter a number of other times.

From 1954 until now Turcato's style has become richer and more refined, but it no longer changes, it progressively frees itself from representation, and develops greater, full-throated energy.

Quadro africano has a purple background with pugnacious white inserts edged with browns, yellows, orange tones, and some greens. This painting shows that Turcato has gained a new strength, faith in himself, and that he has taken a definite and defiant revolutionary position.

Filamenti gialli and *Bacche rosse* are more delicate paintings. The background of the former is gray and pale blue with a web of yellow filaments interwoven with gray. It is obvious that the artist spurns space in depth; but the surface is not merely decorative; there are values expressed through an imagination that delights in uncontrasted passages. In the gray-white and pale blue background of *Bacche rosse*, red shapes threaded with dark gray flow like a stream of blood. The prevailing tones are white and red, colors that represent moments of relaxation, serenity, and happiness.

Reticolo shows an aggressive state of mind and a spirit full of movement, with blood-red shapes on top of white and edged with white and tan. Turcato repeated this web pattern several times in order to show how often he was the prey of nerves.

Mosche cinesi (Plate 43) is less abstract, although it does not in any way represent flies. The pattern is supplied by quick touches of color that arise from a group of leaves and contrast with the golden brown background. These touches might be electric sparks or evil spirits in flight.

122

PLATE 48 - *Composizione,* 1957

Scoppio di maschere, in the Canali Collection, Rome, (Plate 44) is a fine painting. The background consists of a range of delicate grays against which there is a cloud of deeper gray broken up by an explosion of reds and yellows with strong black towards the center. The cloud follows the flight of the imagination and supplies a high quality of painting that goes beyond the pleasant pattern within the same matière, which is as delicate as that of a fresco.

The many paintings Turcato produced in 1957 express enthusiasm and happiness. *Deserto dei Tartari* (Plate 45) has a neutral sandy background covered with touches of pale blue, red, and white that are tortured and dynamic, as if they were plants attempting to struggle out of the desert soil.

Pianta notturna shows gray flowers touched with green and yellow, colors of an enchanting purity against a black background, an expression of the silence of the night. *Migrazione* consists of small areas of white, brown and yellow that the artist's imagination sees as elegant, dynamic, and self-assured migrating birds against a light green background. *Composizione* of 1957 (Plate 46) is very brilliant in colors. *Composizione*, also of 1957, (Plate 48) is a pattern in various shades of brown that weave in and out and thrust themselves upwards over a white background. *Arcipelago*, 1958, (Plate 47) consists of red blotches spreading over a two-tones background in white and gray.

These are extremely fine paintings. Although before 1957 there was some doubt concerning Turcato on account of his tentative style and small production, one must now recognize that he is an artist of the first importance, sure of himself and richly creative.

SCIALOJA

TOTI SCIALOJA

Scialoja is famous for having changed his approach to painting many times but this is no reason to feel doubts about him, such as those voiced by his "friends" and by art dealers; he has been changeable because he has stuck to his own ideas rather than followed current taste, as a glance at his work will clearly prove. Of course, Scialoja's personality is complex. First of all his classical education and his undeniable literary and critical gifts have, on the one hand, benefited his pictorial philosophy; on the other, they have prevented him for a long time from understanding that art today is neither classical nor literary. He realized this in 1953 when he abandoned writing and gave himself entirely to painting. Naturally, he started to write again later on, but by then his experience as a painter had immunized him.

In the past Scialoja also suffered from mistaken ideas concerning the artistic personality, an error made by many Italian critics. They consist in a fierce distrust of current fashions and a belief that joining a group obliterates the artistic personality. There are critics that state with the authority of philosophers that all "isms," whether romantic or Gothic, impressionist or expressionist, are a hindrance to the individual artist's understanding. It is rather as if a study of fourteenth century Italian hindered an understanding of Dante's language. Foolish ideas that do a lot of harm and influence young artists, particularly gifted ones, to overemphasize their individualism. It is perfectly easy, however,

PLATE 49
Speranze perdute, 1955
De Luca Collection, Rome

to be original without being isolated. In fact, those who row together will make greater headway in their battle against the current.

It was Scialoja's fate rather than his fault that he felt the need of splendid isolation. Anyone born in 1914, and reaching the age of twenty at the time of the Fascist empire,

127

who spontaneously decided to be an anti-Fascist, who had the usual literary education but was self-taught as a painter, who, between the ages of twenty-three and thirty, fought first as a soldier and then as a member of the Resistance, would be fatally bound to proclaim his individual attitude and opposition to everything and everybody. And it is due to the generosity and the Italian amiability of Scialoja's nature that after working on his own, impervious to outside influence, he finally chose to join the main stream, where he found himself in good company.

Scialoja's literary culture and family background have lent a refinement to his way of living. Refinement in living has produced outstanding results in art, as in the Venice of the eighteenth century, or the Paris of the 'nineties. In other periods, however, a man of refinement is lost. This has been proved over and over again throughout history. French painting revived in 1905 when it felt the need to exclaim: "Who will save us from people of refinement?" In 1945 a similar necessity arose in Italy with unavoidable results. It may become a moral necessity for everyone to stick together.

Scialoja's sensuality and his emotions saved him from going too far. He knows how to formulate his theories with impeccable logic, but in paint he expresses them in a totally different way, because in painting he feels compelled to convey his emotions rather than his thoughts, and this is exactly what makes him an original artist. His way of feeling, or rather his way of being that makes no distinction between the physical and the spiritual, has proved an unreasonable but effective solution to all the contradictory ideas at work in his mind. He took a tremendous fancy to Jacques Villon, whom he met in Paris in 1947 and 1948, and wrote an enthusiastic article about him. After his stay in Paris there was a change in his painting, but not along Villon's line. This proves that Scialoja does not paint what he wants but what he "must"; on account of his continual wavering, it is not possible to pinpoint his exact stand, but one can grasp that the general process consists in gradually freeing himself from every preconceived idea. The main preconceived ideas which Scialoja left behind through his concentration on painting alone are the compulsory representation of physical objects — even though these could be twisted as much as one wished — and the Italian tradition, or rather the exalted Roman accent given to Expressionism and the elimination of nature in Surrealism. The artist himself has written:

"Painting became second nature to me... I never look at what I have done before, nor think about what I will do tomorrow. I can only say that a given vision, a given discovery, cannot be worked out in just one painting but requires rather a whole series. I am not looking for a formula that will make it easier for me to be understood or to gain recognition. My conception of myself does not come before the painting; I attempt to clarify my vision of the world by exposing it on canvas. My paintings are not autobiographical, they represent my discoveries."

128

PLATE 50   *Sonno grigio*, 1956 Viviano Collection, New York

In 1940 Scialoja held his first show in Genoa. It consisted entirely of drawings and was a polite and discreet first appearance before the public, in which he displayed painterly qualities similar to those of Ranzoni. A year later he exhibited paintings at the Società Amici dell'Arte in Turin. I have seen two of his 1940 paintings, *Cardi e cipolle*

129

PLATE 51   *Procida*, 1957 Lawrence Lader Collection, New York

PLATE 52

Due Rossi, 1957 Museum Art, Denver

and *Teste di agnelli*; theirs is a kind of Expressionism at its most violent, with colors that are still crude. Bleeding lambs are displayed on a white platter resting on a pale blue and green table against a yellow background; Scialoja seems to have been inspired by Ensor.

The style of *Natura morta*, 1942, in the Rome National Gallery of Modern Art, is unchanged, although the colors are quieter and the form more rhythmic.

In *Nudino*, 1943, one feels the influence of Van Gogh concentrated into a decorative

131

pattern. Mafai's influence, and that of the Roman school in general, to which Scialoja adds an additional quality of vibrant Expressionism, can be seen in such paintings of towns as *Paesaggio di Roma*, 1943, in the Ignazio Scimone Collection, Rome. This vibrant quality takes the form of sprightly, decorative contours, as in *Natura morta*, 1944, in the Enrico Scialoja Collection, Rome. In *Procida*, 1945, the houses are represented pleasantly and delicately; one sees the care that has been expended, but they lack vitality.

The need of escaping from the representation of the physical object can already be noted in two paintings of 1946, both entitled *Fabbriche sul Tevere*, one in the Antonio Calvi Collection and the other in the Giovanni Macchia Collection, Rome. An exasperated synthesis removes any real consistence from the image to the advantage of the color harmony, which is no longer so gross.

Pollo spennato, 1947, in tones of pink and red on a dark green background, marks a step forward. Scialoja is perturbed and unfortunately expresses this perturbation in the manner of Soutine, who admittedly was a great artist but a very bad example to follow and one that did a lot of harm.

Even the views of Paris painted in 1948 show this perturbation in their form, which soon loses its spontaneity and becomes mannerism. *L'Opera*, *Baracconi*, *Metro sopraelevato*, belong to this period, in which the artist's experiments with intense color harmonies were successful and obtained a value of their own.

The following year, 1949, the arbitrary tortured contours have disappeared, but the fruits of his experiments with color remain, together with a decisive leaning towards abstraction, where the influence of Picasso vies with that of the Surrealists. *Bagnante* is merely an outline without construction, shades of rose and pale blue against a darker blue background. There is greater constriction and volume in *Natura morta*, carried out in yellowish white on a background of pure yellow, in the Michele Gandin Collection, Rome.

After another trip to Paris in 1950 his images become stronger with contrasting dark and light areas and tonal harmonies, such as in *Paesaggio di Parigi* in the Luigi Magnani Collection, Rome. The analysis derives from Cubism, but the presence of the subject checks the artist's development. This can be observed in *Pecora morta*, 1950, where the flight of the terrified girl requires a technique of illustrative lines that have nothing in common with Cubism, whereas the body of the animal is already dissected in the cubist manner.

Scialoja did not plunge hastily into Cubism. His approach was tentative and reserved. *Bambine in riva al mare*, 1952, still shows the movement of images, although these are only sketched in between geometrical areas, but the effect is too linear to be truly cubist. The transformation of forms, however, is pleasing and original. The colors, inspired by Paul Klee, have become delicate and transparent and have the fairytale quality of the subject; it is the colors, in fact, that have begun to dominate the whole composition. *Il Tamburino* and *Arlecchino*, 1952, in the De Luca Collection, Rome, are examples of his culminating point in the surrealist direction. They fail to be works of art, because the painter's imaginative freedom is still fettered by over-refinement.

The treatment of the objects in *Natura morta*, 1952, is vague and mystical. The agressiveness of *Testa viola*, from the early part of 1953, and *Uomo che dorme*, in the Giorgio Bassani Collection, show that Scialoja had already completely got rid of his preconceived ideas and over-refinement. From now on he can devote himself to his autonomous form and even temporarily give up his use of intensive color in order to blend it better with the forms he has adopted.

Throughout 1954 Scialoja worked intensively on harmonizing planes in space, brought to the surface according to the analytical manner of Cubism. *Luce d'autunno*, a painting of 1954, is one of his most successful examples, with its light and luminous tones of silvery white, dove gray, and yellow. These are contrasted with a series of dark and nocturnal effects. One immediately feels that, in Cubism, Scialoja has found himself and that he no longer needs stimulation from without nor psychological distress within. All he needs is to establish his formal relationships and to carry them out in color. Without his realizing it they themselves will express his state of mind. The year 1954 was a happy moment in Scialoja's life, but a temperament such as his cannot call a halt.

In 1955 Scialoja passed from Cubism to abstract art, that is to say to the representation of an image rather than its physical reality. There is no longer any formal system of disarticulation and reconstruction, as in Cubism, but spontaneous adhesion to images that rise to the surface of consciousness, to forgotten memories, or even to the unknown. This is the manner that I have defined abstract-concrete, in order to indicate that Scialoja's ideal, which is shared by his fellow painters, tends neither to the geometry nor to the architecture of forms but to reality, which is no less real being spiritual and imaginative.

Scialoja's favorite subject, a vision of the past transformed into the present, inspired a series of paintings similar to a theme with variations. *Ricordo di caccia*, 1955, in the Carnegie Institute, Pittsburgh, is a typical example. No episode is depicted, but dark strokes against a light background afford a dramatic contrast and convey his need for energy and ruggedness.

In *Il sonno*, in the Alberto Burri Collection, Rome, another subject of 1955, the form identifies itself perfectly with the light which streams down; the color effect is very fine, although almost monochrome.

Speranze perdute, in the De Luca Collection, Rome, (Plate 49) shows a crisscross of reds against a dark background. These paintings spring from and appeal to sensory perceptions; they do not try to convey precise words or images, but they are moving because

PLATE 53

Pan pi, 1958

an expression of feeling is all the more comprehensive and deep when it is less confined and precise.

A new direction develops in 1956. Scialoja attacked the color problem with the project of making it lighter and more expressive, occasionally giving up space in depth,

PLATE 54   *Impronta ripetuta*, 1958 Odyssia A. Skouras Collection, Rome

as in *Primavera difficile*, of March, 1956, where there are nervous strokes on top of the color masses which have a value of their own. Another example is *Ancora un sonno*, a pale blue and brown pattern on a rosy background, and last of all, *Sonno grigio* in the Viviano Collection, New York, (Plate 50) where the pinkish yellow stands out in contrast to the dark gray. The plastic consistency provides an image although not a likeness.

Scialoja's words explain what his color means to him today:

"Color has begun to lose its allusive feeling and to become a presence, almost physical reality. It is restoring to its primary importance the problem of matière and pictorial surface.

"Before lines were used, painting was the tangible layer; it was whitewash, plaster, hemp, resin, dust, enamel, and crumbled matter. A fiber with pores, in fact. This physical reality goes to make the image together with the color. It is the color itself and the presence of the color. Not shadow or memory or relic, but the complete presence. The pictorial image steadily becomes less an image painted thing but simply *is* in its quality of reality, in its presence on our imagination, and in its resemblance."

In 1956 Toti Scialoja was in New York for a particularly successful exhibition of his works, and he felt encouraged to throw himself intensely into his work on his return. America for him was a lesson in liberty, even in painting, and of conscientiousness from a moral standpoint.

Two of Scialoja's 1957 paintings are illustrated here: *Due rossi*, in the Denver Art Museum, (Plate 52) is a good example of his rebellion against the continuous pattern that was normal in 1956 and was a part of the tradition. By breaking up the pattern, with the reds opening on a white background that is worked in a painterly manner, attention is centered on the dominating red, giving value to the matière and formal dynamism.

Il grido also has a reddish pattern that suggests a fantastic monster moving against a whitish background. In *Dentro il nero*, in the Luisa Spagnoli Collection, Rome, he attempts to show a descent into hell, from which some nocturnal lights gleam forth. *Irritazione* and *Il presente*, in the Giorgio Franchetti Collection, Rome, both painted in 1957, consist of apparitions of black and brown or brown and yellow marks against a light background. The tonal relationships between pattern and background are extremely subtle. The importance of pictorial matière as a motivation for art has become an increasingly important factor in Scialoja's artistic production. I will cite *Alle cinque di sera*, *Metamorfosi*, in the Diebold Collection, New York, *Il segno rosso*, and above all *Procida*, 1957, in the Lawrence Lader Collection, New York, (Plate 51) where a new feeling of relaxation, of joy of vibrant color can be observed. Scialoja likes to stress affinities between pattern and color harmonies, because through concentration on the matière he realizes that it will be ever new and different, like all living things. He

136

took another step towards freeing his imagination in the summer of 1957, which he spent at Procida. One can see developments of his new tendency and his cosmic color in *Pan Pi* (Plate 53), and in *Impronta ripetuta* in the Odyssia A. Skouras Collection, Rome, (Plate 54). Both these paintings date from 1958. It must be recognized that this painter, who is one of the most cultured and most subtle, finds a way of consciously freeing himself from his intellectualism through matière; as he himself expresses it:

"Painting is the result of a spiritual action that tends to transmit its burden, its human reasoning, to the matière directly; using its working methods and its spontaneous covering of one layer over the other and its elementary way of making impressions. Matière provides a record of man in all his movements and instincts, and even of the tremors of his subconscious. Matière becomes the result of human intervention; a physical substance (of which dimension is the other part), changed and transformed and treated by man in his entire being, both body and spirit. This handling of the matière is conditioned by a desire for clarity and wholeness, for truth concerning oneself. In the ultimate analysis, there is always a rhythm, the distinguishing mark of a particular tempo; but it is formed through a repeated search for truth that is tantamount to moral exploration. Absolute sincerity can become a force of nature. The desire to transmit one's own feelings freely and directly, to search, to establish oneself by means of the matière, or through the surface which is given one as an indestructible part of one's awareness."

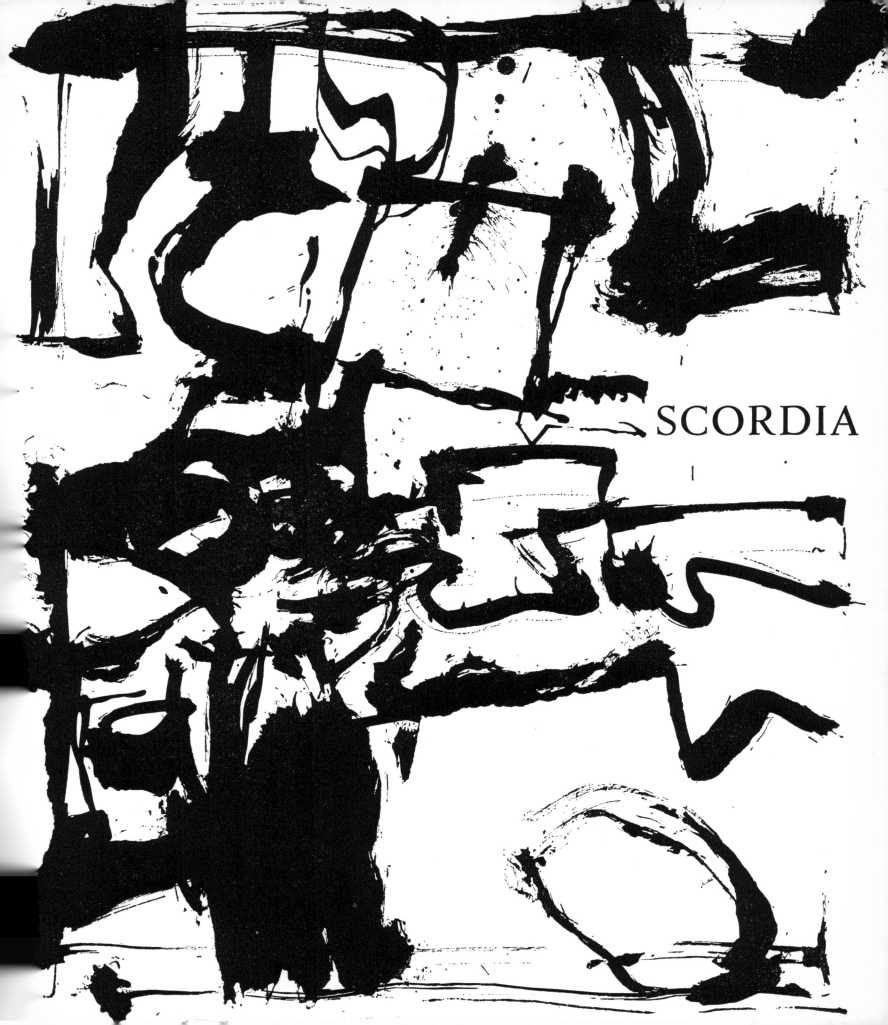

SCORDIA

ANTONIO SCORDIA

Antonio Scordia is a strong-minded man who sticks to his ideas, he faces difficult problems courageously, and he wishes to protest his own personality at all costs. On the other hand his mind is slow, with the result that his progress is more deliberate than that of his fellow artists, although he infallibly reaches his goal. The contrasts in his painting are those he insists on and originate in his quirks of character. His need for a sensuous approach to life leads him to represent natural objects. He then corrects that vision according to the exigencies of his disciplined mind, so that they acquire a stylistic value. In his best works of recent date, this process of elaboration from natural to stylized representation, from the real to the abstract, absorbs the entire painting more and more, and ends with the victory of the style. Natural objects are obviously the basis of each work, but in the end they appear to be mere afterthoughts.

Scordia is not the only artist of his generation to remain attached to natural reality. Cassinari has also been faced with the same problems, and other artists are working along parallel lines. This means that the need for abstraction is the inevitable result of modern life and that the best Italian artists today try to find a relationship between style itself and reproduction, between the abstract and the concrete in painting. The type of painting that we know as abstract-concrete, the French term abstract-impressionist. In Scordia's case, however, one must speak of Expressionism rather than Impressionism.

140

PLATE 55   *Parco d'autunno*, 1956 Campilli Collection, Rome

Scordia was born in the Argentine, at Santa Fé, in 1918 and came to Rome as a child of three, this latter city being his domicile from then onwards. After completing his secondary schooling he went to life classes at the French Academy. He earned his own living, a hard task, and he was very poor. Then came five years of military service, during which he fought in Albania. In 1944 he returned to civil life, completely worn out. But, since drawing had been his passion ever since boyhood, by 1945 he was able to give a one-man show. I have seen *Ritratto con la fidanzata*, 1945, Scordia's last painting in the Roman tonal style, as Kokoschka's Expressionism had influenced him deeply. He carried on with his magazine illustrations and in 1947 had another one-man show. There is a certain force in the arrangement of a portrait of his wife, who is shown stepping forward, large black eyes wide open. His portrait of Gentilini, although painted in a species of Post-Impressionistic style, reflects that tenacious and solid personality that can be seen in Scordia's most recent work. Of the young Roman painters Scordia was considered one of the best, but dealers and collectors treated him with indifference. Scordia decided to try the Argentine and went off to Buenos Aires, where he stayed two years;

141

he had bad luck, no success whatsoever, he took to using exaggerated form and color and was well content when he was able to get back to Rome and his own circle.

Two important events influencing the development of taste had taken place during the two years he was absent from Italy: the *Fronte Nuovo delle Arti* and the 1948 Biennale. Scordia felt that his fellow artists had left him behind them, and in order to catch up he took trips to London and Paris in the years 1949 and 1950. He finally was able to experience the paintings of Cézanne, Braque, Picasso, and Matisse directly. They made him realize that he must study their revolutionary visual approach. It was at this point that he discovered his personal interpretation of Cubism, where the pattern arises from patches and colors in juxtaposition on the surface, with hints at depth. *Valentina* in the De Luca Collection, Rome, *Gatto sulla seggiola* in the National Gallery of Modern Art, Rome, and *Bagnanti*, which he exhibited at the 1952 Biennale, are examples of this period. It is superficial Cubism which he accepts very cautiously, and it may therefore be said that this painter's style only attains maturity in 1953.

In *Donna alla finestra*, shown at the 1954 Biennale, the image is present, but it is well absorbed in the construction of the abstract areas of color. The pattern is pale blue surrounded by brown; the color is kept low but it is rich and has deep overtones. *Natura morta col vassoio*, of the same year, displays greater energy in the use of color — orange-yellows on a pale violet-blue. The central pattern of *Natura morta con teiera bleu*, another painting of 1953, is organized on cubist lines.

The composition of *Ragazza e marinaio* and *Uomo a cavallo*, 1953, both exhibited at the 1954 Biennale, is more complicated, with the object of obtaining richer effects in a cubist manner. Of his 1954 production the following paintings should be mentioned: *L'interno*, where the chair, the table and the model are all handled with a similar distribution of color areas; *Natura morta con caffettiera*, with its beautiful tonal contrasts; and particularly *Donna col macinino da caffè*, where there is a hint of the style that Scordia will develop later on; that is to say, the areas of color on the surface and the simplified forms are broken up in a way that arouses the imagination of the viewer and gives a mysterious force to the fragments of the image.

Stylistic uncertainties disappear in 1954, with the result that Scordia's nine works exhibited at the 1955 Quadriennale place him once again on a par with the best Italian painters. As he himself has written, this is the beginning of a period of "greater richness and freedom... From now on my relationship with reality takes a different turn. The exultation that arises from certain aspects of reality turn it into a more freely subjective vision; and even if my attention has remained fixed on a world of phenomena, I attempt to find a plastic equivalent to the many emotions aroused by intense involvement. This is how I build up my world of images.

PLATE 56   *Interno*, 1956 De Luca Collection, Rome

PLATE 57

Paesaggio notturno, 1957

PLATE 58   *Gita al Faro*, 1957

"I have been working along these lines during the last two years and reacquiring my natural spontaneity, seeking out ways of representing my constant need for expressing feeling through color and the use of strongly constructed space and avoiding any facile spirit of rebellion or any preconceived ideas."

Two 1955 paintings, *Gallo* and *Donna col cesto*, where the pattern consists of broken forms, are good examples of the way he has freed his imagination. He uses these broken forms more and more frequently. They play a dominating role and serve to accentuate

145

PLATE 59   *Concerto*, 1957 Pogliani Gallery, Rome

PLATE 60

Il Grande Sipario, 1958

the color contrasts. The blacks and reds in *Gallo* are colors used as a function of the abstract light. The image is still present but seems to become lost in some distant age of fable. In *Cavallo rosso*, 1955, in the Hudson Collection, New York, the broken forms are completely absorbed by the color effects, which are expanded to wider areas; the over-all effect is obtained by a dark pattern on a lighter background.

Scordia uses this principle of broken forms as a way of giving new vitality to the construction of landscapes, such as *Paesaggio marino; Paesaggio di Londra*, in the Gallery of Modern Art, Macerata; and above all, *Paesaggio con i colombi*, in the Marino Collection, Milan; all of which date from 1955.

He painted *Colazione sull'erba* in 1956, taking Manet's *Déjeuner sur l'herbe* as his starting point. Scordia fits the pattern into abstract elements by strong contrasts. *Cesto di frutta sul mare* has touches of yellow, green and black on a sea-blue background; *Parco d'autunno* in the Campilli Collection, Rome, (Plate 55) has exceptionally fine color because the imaginary composition completely absorbs the pattern. The same holds true of *Interno*, in the De Luca Collection, Rome, (Plate 56) which has a red area that destroys the arrangement of the various planes in space. At this point one might observe that, natural reality having been cast aside, the new painterly reality is the result of the anarchy of abstraction, that is to say of the emotion that breaks up every abstract scheme.

Siesta in campagna, 1956-57, is light in tone, the pretext for the painting being the recumbent figures of a woman clad in white. *Figura sulla veranda*, 1956, shows a red-toned figure on a light background that gives unity to the painting and to the color.

The works that Scordia painted in 1957 for the Sao Paulo exhibition in Brazil are particularly fine, as are those of 1958. *Interno dello studio* has a tonal unity of dark colors on a light background which displays an energy and a disorder that are a part of painterly reality. The formal disorder also gives a great deal of vitality to *Giardino antico*, which has fine color; the foreground of *Spiaggia notturna* is light toned, the background dark. *Paesaggio notturno* (Plate 57) has a pattern in pale blue-gray and red-gray; it is a strong and original work. The color streams over *Ruderi nel parco* in a way that shows Scordia's period of broken forms has come to an end. The color unity is created by dark tones over lighter ones without any set planes, and areas of color are so full of energy that they give the painting a life of its own. By the end of 1957 Scordia's style had become broader and surer. There is even a dynamic effect that reveals inner passion. The contrasting blacks and reds in *Concerto* in the Pogliani Gallery, Rome, (Plate 59) are severe and dramatic. The background of *Gita al Faro* (Plate 58) is rose-colored, giving a light-hearted effect, but the pattern hints at dramatic complications, although the colors are rather light.

Of Scordia's 1958 paintings *Il Grande Sipario* (Plate 60) attracted a good deal of favorable attention at the Rome-New York Art Foundation exhibition.

148

It is easier to predict what line Scordia's fellow artists will take than what he will be doing in the future. It is obvious that he is painting better at present than he was last year, and there is sureness in handling his newly acquired freedom that prevents errors of taste. One thing is certain, he will never accept any new suggestion without weighing it carefully. The conscientiousness of his attitude towards his art is exemplary. But he will not be satisfied with the results he has obtained so far; with deliberate stead-fastness he will seek to improve himself further.

VEDOVA

EMILIO VEDOVA

A boy prodigy who at sixteen has already been acclaimed by the public should by all the rules have no future whatsoever. But Vedova has a perfect antidote to the dangers of success and self-satisfaction. He throws himself into the fray both as a man and as an artist and frees himself in a cataclysmic manner from all barriers and starts on his way to the unknown all over again. He thinks he knows exactly where he is going, and he takes greater pains to reach his goal than do many of his better fellow artists. No wonder he exaggerates, but he even finds the remedy against the excesses of an unbridled personality and passionate agitation, which consists of work itself on a craftsmanship basis, carried out unceasingly and patiently and that acts as a brake on the imagination. Manual dexterity, a violent sense of freedom, and the discipline imposed by art are the three things that go to form the rhythm of Vedova's life.

He was born in Venice in 1919, where his family were craftsmen in a modest way, and although his father realized his son's aptitude for painting, Emilio Vedova at eleven years old was sent to work as an apprentice at a workshop specializing in enamel decorations. His work was hard, but in the evenings he went to the school of design, where, however, he never succeeded in learning to paint water colors without spots or understanding geometry. He lost his job after an argument with his employer; in the meantime he had become extremely run down through excessive work; once he was better he found a job with a photographer, but he couldn't get along with him either. He tried

152

PLATE 61

Crocifissione, 1953 National Gallery of Modern Art, Rome

to lacquer wood objects but this too was an unsuccessful venture. He started to study again but failed to obtain the diploma of elementary school teacher, and after that he worked for a short time as a gilder of picture frames. Emilio was too restless to work steadily. After being apprenticed to the restorer Zenaro, he went to work for Zampa, a violent and apocalyptic painter with one leg who slept in the storehouse of a fried fish shop and painted outdoors in the daytime in order to provide food not only for himself and his assistant but also for the salesman who hawked his paintings through the streets.

In the meantime Emilio's parents were waiting for some good luck to befall him, as it did, through an aunt who had married a nephew of Antonio Mancini. His uncle Alfredo was struck by some of Emilio's drawings of Venetian churches. He took them with him to Rome, where no one believed that they had been done by a sixteen-year-old boy. He then invited Emilio himself to Rome, and took him to Florence, to see the works of Masaccio, and to Arezzo to pay his respects to Piero della Francesca. Before arriving in Rome at his villa in the Terme Deciane, which was full of memories of the great Antonio Mancini, Emilio's uncle clothed him, took care of him, got him

153

back into shape after his hardships, and took him to see Carlo Siviero, who after a good look at his drawings advised the boy to take life classes without seeking admittance to the Academy. The boy prodigy soon gained recognition outside the family circle, and Guido Guida wrote an article in praise of him in the August, 1937, edition of *Illustrazione Vaticana*. The formality of his surroundings made Emilio feel uncomfortable, and after a year he went off to Venice, turning his back on a life of ease. His Mancini uncle and aunt continued to help him for a short period, although they were annoyed because he had taken up the study of philosophy at the Marciana Library instead of sticking to painting. They stopped sending him money when they decided he had dropped painting completely.

At this point Vedova found a friend, Hermann Pircher of Bolzano, who got a large enough allowance from home to keep the pair of them. They went to Florence together in order to paint in the surrounding countryside and to meditate in that city on Savonarola, Giotto and Masaccio. Vedova remembers this period as one of the happiest of his life. Both the young men got to know anti-Fascists and were affected by social conditions. They wanted to represent poverty in their paintings. Pircher told Emilio about German Romanticism. He had him to stay at his home in Bolzano and awakened in him a love for forests and for nature in general. They parted because Emilio had become increasingly nervous and was given to emotional outbursts. On his return to Venice, Vedova obtained a studio through the Bevilacqua Foundation in the attic of a ruined palace. He ate in a restaurant below where they allowed him to charge his meals. He exhibited at the Artists' Trade Union Show in 1941, where another painter, Cesetti, encouraged him. He then went to Milan where he met Morlotti and took part in the 1942 Bergamo Prize competition and exhibited at the Corrente Gallery. Rouault and Vlaminck had made a great impression in artistic circles, which were now roused by Picasso's *Guernica*. He also joined in the activities of the anti-Fascist anarchists. Vedova helped draw up a revolutionary manifesto at Raffaele De Grada's house, and when the latter was put in prison Vedova succeeded in hiding the proofs of the manifesto and returning to Venice. There are some traces of those tumultuous times left in his pattern of speech. At the moment of the Italian debacle Vedova went first to Florence and then to Rome and finally, with Turcato, returned to the country around Belluno. Then he took part in the Resistance and was wounded. When he got back to Venice he had to return to the hospital, as he had left the Belluno hospital too soon, but at last he survived.

He was one of the founders of the *Fronte Nuovo delle Arti*, which began October 1, 1946 — a brief episode, since Togliatti used a reproduction of one of Vedova's paintings to illustrate the type of art he felt unacceptable. For several years he led an unsettled life, full of artistic and social upheavals. In the meantime painters and

PLATE 62   *Anime prigioniere*, 1951 Festa Collection, Vicenza

collectors had gradually become interested in his work.   Arturo Martini suddenly gave him a prize, and Breddo took him as an example.   He sold paintings, made money, spent it immediately, but he didn't want to pay taxes.   He took photographs of his paintings to the tax collector who was horrified, and, in the belief that Vedova's paintings were unsalable, he struck Vedova's name from the income tax collector's list.   His *Sturm und Drang* period ended in 1951, and a new era of serenity and hard work

155

began when he got married. From then on Vedova has disappeared into private life, and his public activities are only connected with his painting.

The pen and ink drawings Vedova made in 1935 when he was sixteen were meant to represent Venetian churches such as SS. Giovanni e Paolo and the Salute. In *Interno della chiesa dei Frari*, for example, light and shade are magnificently organized, and the painting not only shows a sureness of style exceptional in a sixteen-year-old but also is a forerunner of that mature style that can be seen, for instance, in *Città ostaggio*, painted in 1954. Vedova still believed in perspective in 1935, and his luminous rhythm has a basis in reality; by 1954, on the other hand, spatial arrangement does not precede luminous rhythm but is absorbed by it. The difference may seem infinitesimal, but, in order to reach this new viewpoint, Cubism, Futurism, the whole of modern art, had to be experienced. Tintoretto more than any other painter had aroused Vedova's desire to paint, and Piranesi's etchings had inspired his architectural drawings.

By 1942 Vedova's painting had undergone a fundamental change. In *Cantiere alla Giudecca* in the Seno Collection, Venice, for instance, there is barely enough simplification to indicate reality. The formal construction successfully conveys the feeling of discomfort and fear Vedova felt at the sight of the yards. The color has a brand new intensity. *Caffeuccio Veneziano*, exhibited at the Corrente Gallery and now in the Camerino Collection, Venice, dates from the same year and shows Rouault's influence, both in the distortion of the faces and in the manner of handling the pigment; Vedova was acquainted with Rouault only through reproductions. *Vendemmia* in the Dalla Villa Collection, Lendinara, also belongs to this period. His arrangement of forms is freer and the color has become brilliant with bursts of yellow on a pale blue background.

Vedova had painted religious pictures, and used himself as a model for Christ in the Via Crucis. The apocalyptic and catastrophic nature of the theme suited him, and when he realizes that he was not the only one to suffer, that there are so many unfortunate people in this world, he supposes himself to be, like Permeke, the painter of the poor. He reads Dostoyevsky, and Lorenzo Viani arouses his enthusiasm. He gazes on Goya and Daumier and gets to know *Guernica* through reproductions.

Finally the end of the war arrives. Vedova immediately feels the necessity for abstract experiments and to start painting in the new manner. In studying the new relationships between space and areas in order to reach harmonies of pure form, he overcomes all the materialisms that were latent in the expressionistic vein, in the continual wish to rebel that had shown itself during the war. *Immagine del tempo* 1947, in the Natale Collection, Rome, is a good example of this state of mind, of this expe-

156

PLATE 63   *Dal ciclo della natura, I*, 1956 Private Collection, Brazil

rience, which has disciplined his painting and given him time for reflection and for deliberate investigation of formal composition.

The German Romanticism he had discovered through his friend Pircher, and his natural need for occasional outbursts, made it natural for Vedova to combine the study of abstract form with violence of expression. Whereas *Pescatore Adriatico*, 1946-47, and *Cucitrice*, 1946-51, in the Catherine Viviano Collection, New York, are above all a balanced arrangement of lines; *Comizio*, 1946, in the Schettini Collection, Milan, shows lines in a vibrant conflict, like a clash of ideas. *L'Uragano*, 1948, in the Jesi Collection, Milan, shows broken forms whirling and colliding violently, although dominated and sealed into the whole. His *Trittico della Libertà*, 1949, like the Beckmann triptych in the Museum of Modern Art, New York, shows an obsession with the cruelty of war. *La Lotta*, 1949, in the Bonomi Collection, Sao Paulo, conveys a sense of spiritual exasperation through a way of painting which, although it wishes to be calm and objective, remains raw and unfinished in spite of the obvious desire to express light through a careful selection of pale and darker colors.

The evolution of Vedova's style from 1951 onwards proceeds more slowly, although he works at it as hard as ever but without the rabid spirit of earlier years. His artistic experience has widened, his trips to Paris, Brazil, and Germany, the successes and the prizes he has won, have all contributed to give him a new confidence in himself and to make him intensely preoccupied by his work. Although only forty, he is already a celebrated master, sought out both in Europe and America. In Paris in 1951 he felt the need to abolish his straight lines, to use such curves as were required to express impetuous motion, and to find a way of introducing infinite space into the relationship of light and shade. He was inspired by such subjects as *Ballo*, in the Nino Festa Collection, Vicenza, where the blacks are dribbled on to the canvas in order to give them the same tonal value as the background. *Immagine del Tempo*, in the Schettini Collection, Milan, *Energie Scatenate* in the Nino Festa Collection, Vicenza, *Battaglia*, in the Ph. A. Bruno Collection, New York, *Anime prigioniere* in the Nino Festa Collection, Vicenza, (Plate 62) all of 1951, display painterly values, as if Vedova, after a long attachment to Mondrian, had suddenly looked again at Tintoretto.

His new interest in life, his optimism, and his faith in the future freed Vedova from his former excessive preoccupation with geometrical form that made him timid about his own work. Since he and his painting are all of a piece, his *joie de vivre* now finds expression as light and space evolving out of his forms.

But the needs of painting as such once more took the upper hand; Vedova refused to allow pictorial values to deteriorate into mere color effects. As a result he painted a series of pictures from which color is almost banished, and blacks and whites dominate almost the entire canvas. It appears as if he were afraid to lose himself in color and

PLATE 64   *Lettera aperta*, 1957 Campilli Collection, Rome

had felt the need to curtail his means of expression in order to give full freedom to his tumultuous passions. Without doubt some of his best compositions have been carried out in black and white. *Immagine del tempo-Miniera*, in the Festa Collection, Vicenza, *Aggressività incombente No. 1*, shown at the 1952 Biennale, *Esplosione* and *Battaglia Navale*, in the Pierre Gallery, Paris, *Visione Cosmica* in the Guggenheim Collection, Venice, all of 1952, should be mentioned as among Vedova's severest masterpieces, even if an excessive and voluntary self-mortification is occasionally revealed by this stringency. Perhaps *Invasione*, in the Cavellini Collection, Brescia, illustrates better than any other painting of 1952 the severe way in which he expressed raging passion; it manifests through abstract forms the desperate sensation of someone overcome by an invading force. It is certain that the blacks are steel and that the lights reveal depths of tragedy.

1953 is a good year for his painting. It is clear that he feels more keenly the need for a third dimension. *Dal ciclo della natura, No. 9*, in the Civic Museum of Turin, and *Palmaria*, in the Hoogendiyk Collection, Amster-

PLATE 65 - *Immagine del tempo, IV,* 1957
Cavellini Collection, Brescia

PLATE 66

Diario, 1957

dam, are landscapes, but with forms that have never existed in nature but could be found there and could, in any case, have been "seen" by the imagination. We have come far from regular abstract painting; the cycle of development is now complete. Vedova's dramatic spirit finds a grandiose realization in his *Crocifissione*, 1953, exhibited at the University of Trieste in December, 1953, and considered by experts to be the best picture in that show; it now hangs in the National Gallery of Modern Art, Rome, (Plate 61). *Tumulto* and other paintings belonging to the *Ciclo della protesta* and to *Ciclo della natura*, all of 1953, are among Vedova's best works.

He lightened some of his patterns in 1954 and substituted a diffuse and beautiful gray tone, which expresses the serene state of mind the artist had attained, for the former extreme contrasts of black and white. He becomes interested in the beauty of the matière created by the brush through gradations of color and in this way becomes spiritualized. A good example of this is *San Paulo No. 2*, in the Nino Festa Collection, Vicenza. *Spazio inquieto*, in the Giavi Collection, Venice, and *Città ostaggio*, in the Peggy Guggenheim Collection, Venice, both of 1954, are among the most passionate and individual of the tragedies Vedova has painted.

Viaggio in Italia, 1955, the painting which won the Esso Prize, is certainly one of his most successful innovations in the use of color. The reds, yellows, and pale blues ring out among the blacks and whites and become the protagonists of the composition by carrying its movement, both on the surface and in depth. The pattern and the form in color are inseparable; together they reveal the imagination completely detached and intent only on the pleasures of composition.

From 1955 onwards Vedova's painting has not only become rich in spatial intuitions but every now and again overflows with color in a way that formerly was foreign to this painter. *Dal ciclo della natura No. 1*, 1956, Brazil, (Plate 63), *Lettera aperta*, in the Campilli Collection, Rome, (Plate 64), *Immagine del tempo No. 4*, in the Cavellini Collection, Brescia, (Plate 65), and *Diario 1957* (Plate 66), which has a special monumental quality, are examples of the final development of his most recent trend. The patterns are extremely beautiful, and the completely free form dominates the color contribution. The fusion between the pattern and the whole composition is complete. If these paintings are compared with *Anime prigioniere*, 1951, his former attachment to the physical aspects of form can be seen, whereas in his work of 1957 the spiritual expression is more immediate and pure. It seems that Vedova has now fulfilled a wish that he has had for years, not only to express his own emotions but also to express them in harmony with the spirit of the universe. Vedova has reached a very high creative level through his diversity of interests, his indomitable courage, his mastery of his art, and his greater responsiveness to other people's point of view. He is only forty, and we may expect that he will astonish us still further.

BIOGRAPHIES AND BIBLIOGRAPHIES
OF THE INDIVIDUAL PAINTERS

FAUSTO PIRANDELLO

Born in Rome, 1899, and a resident of that city. He followed the classic curriculum, and did not attend the Academy of Fine Arts. He exhibited for the first time at the Venice Biennale in 1926, and in 1928 went to Paris; he held his first one-man show at the Vildrac Gallery in the following year. From then on he has exhibited in various one-man shows in the main cities of Europe and America, and his work has been shown in the most important exhibitions of Italian art. He has won many prizes: at the Rome Quadriennale in 1935 and 1939, and in 1952 when he obtained the most important award; he obtained also the Taranto Prize in 1950, the Fiorino Prize in 1956, and many others. His works are hung in the National Gallery of Modern Art in Rome, as well as in Turin, Milan, Palermo, Detroit, and in many other public and private collections, both in Italy and abroad.

Writings by Pirandello:

Presentazione. (Introduction). Catalogue for the III Quadriennale, Rome, 1939.

Quaderno d'arte. (An art notebook). Quadrivio, Rome, March-December, 1942.

Lettera confessione. (Confession in letter form). Educazione politica, June 20, 1949.

Appunti. (Notes). Monograph by Virgilio Guzzi. Published by De Luce, Rome, 1950.

Dal Diario. (Extracts from a diary). Botteghe Oscure, vol. IX, Rome, 1952.

Dal Diario. (Extracts from a diary). Letteratura, N. 2, Rome, 1953.

La gambe dei Bizantini. (The legs of the Byzantines). La Fiera Letteraria, Rome, January 8, 1956.

Klee Figurativo. (Klee as a figurative artist). La Fiera Letteraria, Rome, October 14, 1956.

Ordini Imponderabili. (Imponderable orders). La Fiera Letteraria, Rome, April 7, 1957.

Taccuino. (Notebook). La Fiera Letteraria, Rome, July 21, 1957.

Cavolo, Misura e Senso. (Cabbage, measure and meaning). La Fiera Letteraria, Rome, May, 25, 1958.

Natura dell'oggetto operante. (Nature of the forming object). La Fiera Letteraria, Rome, July 10, 1958.

Bibliography:

WARNOD A.: *Pirandello.* Comoedia, Paris, March 8, 1929.

ROGER-MARX C.: *Pirandello.* Europe Nouvelle, Paris, March 16, 1929.

FRANCINI A.: *Pirandello.* L'Italia Letteraria, Rome, May, 1931.

MELLI R.: *Pirandello.* Il Tevere, Rome, March 24, 1934.

CECCHI E.: *Pirandello alla II Quadriennale.* (Pirandello at the II Quadriennale). Circoli, Roma, March 1935.

GIUSTI.: *Pirandello.* Corrente di Vita Giovanile, Milan, December 15, 1939.

MASELLI E.: *Pirandello.* Maestrale, Rome, 1942.

VALSECCHI M.: *Pirandello.* Libro e Moschetto, Milan, March, 1942.

BELLONZI F.: *Pirandello.* Domenica, Rome, December 10, 1944.

DE LIBERO L.: *Pittura di Fausto Pirandello*. (The painting of Fausto Pirandello). Quadrante, Rome, December, 1944.

ALVARO C.: *Nuovi quadri di Fausto Pirandello*. (New paintings by Fausto Pirandello). Catalogue for the show at the Galleria del Secolo, Rome, February 9, 1947.

GUZZI V.: *Fausto Pirandello*. Published by De Luca, Rome, 1950

DE LIBERO L.: *Pirandello all'inferno*. (Pirandello and Hell). Letteratura N. 2, Rome, March-April, 1953.

VENTURI L.: *Fausto Pirandello*. Commentari, vol. I, Rome, 1954.

PONENTE N.: *Fausto Pirandello*. Taccuino delle arti n. 16, Rome, 1957.

MARIO MAFAI

Born in Rome, 1902, and a resident of that city. He began to exhibit with Scipione in 1928 after attending the British School and the French Academy and the free life classes at Villa Medici. From then on his work was included in all the principal Italian art shows. He won the Bergamo Prize in 1941, the Verona Prize in 1942, the Perugia Prize in 1947, the Pisa Prize in 1948, the Siena Prize and the Colomba Prize in 1949, and the Rome Quadriennale Prize, 1955-56. His works are hung in the National Gallery of Modern Art in Rome, and in the Sao Paulo Museum, as well as in many private collections, both in Italy and abroad.

Writings by Mario Mafai:

Arte Nuova a Parigi. (New art in Paris). L'Italia Letteraria, Rome, August 31, 1930.

La pittura parigina. (Parisian painting). L'Italia Letteraria, Rome, October 31, 1930.

In morte di Scipione. (On the death of Scipione). L'Italia Letteraria, Rome, November 19, 1933.

Presentazione alla propria mostra personale. (Introduction for his one-man show). Catalogue for the II Quadriennale, Rome, 1935.

Dichiarazioni sulla Biennale del 1938. (Statements concerning the Biennale of 1938). Quadrivio, Rome, June 12, 1938.

La mia pittura. (My painting). Tempo, Milan, March 7, 1940.

Il pittore, l'uomo, le pere. (The painter, the man and the pears). Prospettive n. 25-27, Rome, 1942.

Sulla pittura. (On painting). Pattuglia n. 7-8, Forlì, 1943.

Pittura d'oggi. (Painting today). Vieusseux Collection, edited by Michelangelo Masciotta, Florence 1945, Page 129.

Lettera all'editore De Luca. (A letter to the publisher De Luca). Monograph edited by Libero de Libero, Rome, 1949.

I ricordi. (Memoirs). Pittori che scrivono, edited by Leonardo Sinisgalli, Milan, 1954, Page 147.

La pittura del 1929. (Painting in 1929). Il Contemporaneo, Rome, May 1, 1954.

Appunti. (Notes). Catalogue for Mafai's one-man show at the Tartaruga Gallery, Rome, February 21, 1955.

Polemica sull'astrattismo. (Controversy on abstract painting). Il Punto, Rome, October 5, 1957.

Bibliography:

DE LIBERO L.: *Ottocento e Novecento a Roma. La tradizione. Mafai e Scipione*. (Nineteenth and twentieth Century art in Rome. The tradition. Mafai and Scipione). Belvedere, Milan, April, 1930.

BERTOCCHI N.: *Il pittore Mario Mafai*. (The painter Mario Mafai). L'Italia Letteraria, Rome, December 2, 1932.

MELLI R.: *Mafai alla Quadriennale*. (Mafai at the Quadriennale). L'Italia Letteraria, Rome, February 16, 1935.

BRANDI C.: *Su alcuni giovani*. (Some young painters). Le Arti, Florence, February-March, 1939.

RAGGHIANTI C. L.: *Mario Mafai*. Introduction for the show at the Arcobaleno Gallery, Venice, August, 1939.

GUTTUSO R.: *Nota a Mafai*. (A letter to Mafai). Primato, Rome, September 1, 1940.

MARCHIORI G.: *Artisti contemporanei: Mario Mafai*. (Contemporary painters: Mario Mafai). Emporium, Bergamo, September, 1940.

BRANDI C.: *Mafai*. Beltempo, Rome, 1942.

MASCIOTTA M.: *Mafai*. Letteratura, Florence, January, 1942.

SCIALOJA T.: *Mafai*. Il Selvaggio, Rome, March 15, 1942.

SANTANGELO A.: *Mafai*. Quaderni del Disegno Contemporaneo, n. 3, Milan, 1943.

ARGAN G. C.: *Mafai*. La Nuova Europa, Rome, December 30, 1945.

MARCHIORI G.: *Mafai*. Paesaggio, Pisa, April, 1946.

DE LIBERO L.: *Mafai*. Published by De Luca, Rome, 1950.

PONENTE N.: *Scipione e il gusto italiano del 1930*. (Scipione and the Italian taste of the thirties). Letteratura n. 8-9, Rome, 1954.

VENTURI L.: *Mario Mafai*. Commentari, vol. I, Rome, 1957.

VENTURI L.: *Mario Mafai*. Introduction to the catalogue for the XXIX Biennale, Venice, 1958.

RENATO BIROLLI

Born in Verona, 1906, died in Milan 1959. He studied at the Cignaroli Academy in Verona, and, as a very young man, joined the Secondo Novecento *(Second Nineteenth Century) group which, however, he abandoned shortly afterwards. He was one of the founders of the* Nuova Secessione Artistica *(New Artistic Secession), which developed into the* Fronte Nuovo delle Arti *(New Art Front). In 1952 he exhibited with the* Gruppo degli otto pittori italiani *(the group of eight). He has had one-man shows both in Italy and abroad and has been represented in all the most important art exhibitions, receiving numerous prizes, among them the Carnegie Prize, Pittsburgh 1955, and the Lissone Prize, 1956. His works are hung in the National Gallery of Modern Art in Rome, in the museums of Modern Art in Paris, and in the museums of Sao Paulo, St. Louis, Kansas City, Buffalo, Pittsburgh, Lyon, Malmo, Stockholm, Ljubljana, Zurich, Tel Aviv, Eilat, and in the Turin, Milan, Venice, and La Spezia Galleries, as well as in many public and private collections.*

Writings by Birolli:

Birolli has written a great deal. Only such works of his that concern his painting or that can shed light on his personality as an artist are listed here.

Pensieri sull'arte. (Reflections on art). Il Ventuno, n. 27, Venice, March 1935.

Teorica d'arte. (Theory of art). Il Ragguaglio, Milan, May 25, 1935.

Teorica d'arte. (Theory of art). Il Morgante, Milan, February, 1936.

Città: con riferimento alla pittura. (The city: with reference to painting). Corrente di Vita Giovanile, Milan, September 30, 1939.

Città: con riferimento a una esperienza: (The City: with reference to an experience). Corrente di Vita Giovanile, Milan, May 15, 1940.

Scritti. (Writings). With a criticism of the text by Sandro Bini, Milan, 1941.

Confessione per un quadro. (Confession concerning a painting). Prospettive, Rome, January 15-March 15, 1942.

Sedici Taccuini. (Sixteen notebooks). With ten drawings and a note by Umbro Apollonio, Novara, 1943.

Come parlare agli uomini. (The way to talk to people). Le Tre Arti, Milan, October 1, 1945.

Non sono che un pittore. (I am only a painter). Venice, Trieste, May-June, 1946.

Idee e informazioni sull'arte contemporanea. (Ideas and information on contemporary art). Lecture held at the Università Popolare, and published in the Voce delle Prealpi, Varese, December 18, 1950.

Italia 1944. (Italy 1944). Edizioni della Conchiglia, Milan, 1952.

Taccuino della Marche (Necropoli Contadina). Notebook from the Marches (a peasant necropolis) Pittori che scrivono, edited by Leonardo Sinisgalli, Milan, 1954.

Conferenze. (Lecture). Pittura d'Oggi, Vieusseux Collection, edited by Michelangelo Masciotta, Florence, 1954.

Patagonia a Sud delle Cinqueterre. (Patagonia, South of Cinqueterre). L'Unità, Milan, February 5, 1955.

Risposte all'inchiesta. (Replies to a survey). Pittura Italiana del dopoguerra, by Tristan Sauvage, published by Schwarz, Milan, 1957, page 312.

Inediti. (Unedited writings). (Letters from 1947 to 1955). Arte Astratta, by Achille Cavellini, Edizioni della Conchiglia, Milan, 1957.

La quinta stagione, and *Taccuini inediti*. (The fifth season and Unedited notebooks). Birolli, edited by Giampiero Giani, Milan, 1958.

Bibliography:

PERSICO E.: *Birolli*, Casabella, Milan, March, 1933.

DE GRADA R.: *Ritratti d'artisti.* (Portraits of artists). L'Italia Letteraria, Rome, October 27, 1935.

BINI S.: *Premessa a Renato Birolli.* (Preliminary notes concerning Renato Birolli). Corrente di Vita Giovanile, Milan, May 15, 1938.

SINISGALLI L.: *Birolli.* Introduction for the catalogue of Birolli's one-man show at the Genova Gallery, October 12-28, 1938.

BINI S.: *Birolli.* Milan, 1941.

PIOVENE G.: *Birolli.* Domus, n. 158, Milan, February, 1941, page 34.

VERONESI G.: *Nota su Birolli.* (Note on Birolli). Le Arti, vol. IV, Milan, April-May, 1941.

ARGAN G. C.: *Renato Birolli.* Catalogue for the first show of the Fronte Nuovo delle Arti, (New Art Front) Milan, 1947.

VALSECCHI M.: *Renato Birolli*. Panorama dell'Arte Italiana, Turin, 1950.

MALTESE C.: *Cultura e realtà nella pittura di Birolli*. (Culture and reality in the painting of Birolli). Commentari, vol. I, Florence, 1950.

BALLO G.: *Birolli o del colore*. (Birolli, or notes on color). Bellezza, Milan, March, 1950.

MALCHIORI G.: *Renato Birolli*. Letteratura, n. 2, Rome, 1954.

VENTURI L.: *Renato Birolli*. Commentari, vol. IV, Rome, 1954.

APOLLONIO U.: *Pittura di Birolli*. (Birolli's painting). Quadrum, n. 1, Bruxelles, May, 1956.

VALSECCHI M.: *Renato Birolli*. Introduction for the catalogue of Birolli's one-man show at the Odyssia Gallery, Rome, March 20, 1958.

GIUSEPPE SANTOMASO

Born in Venice, 1906, and a resident of that city. He studied at the Venice Academy of Fine Arts, and first exhibited his work at the Ca' Pesaro Gallery. In 1937 he traveled in Holland and in France, thereby completing his training as an artist, He was a member of the Fronte Nuovo delle Arti *(New Art Front), and exhibited with them in 1948 at the Venice Biennale, and with the* Gruppo degli otto pittori italiani *(the group of eight) in 1952. He has had numerous one-man shows both in Italy and abroad, and has won many important prizes, among which the Esso Prize, 1951, the Golfo di La Spezia, 1952, and another prize at the Sao Paulo Biennale, 1951. He was also given the Venice Municipal Prize for an Italian painter exhibiting at the XXVII Venice Biennale, and the Marzotto Prize in 1958. His works are to be found in many private collections both in Italy and abroad, at the National Gallery of Modern Art in Rome, and in the museums of Helsinki, Milan, Sao Paulo, Turin, Trieste, Venice, La Chaux-des-Fonds, Boston, Brooklyn, etc. He has illustrated a number of books, including Paul Eluard's "Grand Air", published in Milan in 1945, in Duilio Morosini's translation.*

Writings by Santomaso:

Risposta a Luigi Bartolini. (Reply to Luigi Bartolini). Michelangelo, Milan, 1945.

Il congresso delle arti a Roma. (The arts' congress in Rome). Domani, Venice, February 6, 1946.

Realismo e astrattismo. (Realism and abstractism). Il Mattino del Popolo, Venice, November 13, 1948.

Fine del Fronte Nuovo delle Arti. (The end of the (New Art Front). Cronache Veneziane, Venice, April 9, 1950.

Enquête sur le rêalism socialiste. Reponses des peintres italiens. (Inquiry concerning socialist realism. The Italian painters' answers). Preuves, Paris, July, 1953.

Bibliography:

MARCHIORI G.: *Galleria: Santomaso*. (Gallery Notes: Santomaso). Corriere Padano, Ferrara, November 9, 1938.

MARCHIORI G.: *Santomaso*. Corrente di Vita Giovanile, Milan, April 30, 1939.

PODESTÀ A.: *Bepi Santomaso*. Domus, Milan, March, 1940.

PALLUCCHINI R.: *Bepi Santomaso*. Emporium, Bergamo, May, 1942.

APOLLONIO U.: *Sul pittore Santomaso*. (Concerning Santomaso, the painter). Paesaggio, n. 1, Pisa, April-May, 1946.

VALSECCHI M.: *Santomaso*. Catalogue for the first show of the Fronte Nuovo delle Arti (new art front). Milan, 1947.

DELL'ORO G.: *L'arte ceramica di Giuseppe Santomaso*. (Giuseppe Santomaso's ceramics). Il Gazzettino Illustrato, Venice, June 3, 1949.

HERBERT READ.: *Santomaso*. Introduction to the catalogue for the show at the Hanover Gallery, London, November-December, 1953.

MARCHIORI G.: *Santomaso*. Published by Alfieri, Venice, 1954.

ARGAN G. C.: *Santomaso*. Catalogue for the XXVII Biennale, Venice, 1954.

BREDDO G.: *Santomaso*. Biennale, n. 19-20, Venice 1954.

VENTURI L.: *Bepi Santomaso*. Commentari, vol. II, Rome, 1955.

VON HEILMAIER H.: *Giuseppe Santomaso und die Wandlungen der italienische Malerei*. (Giuseppe Santomaso and the new development of Italian painting). Die Kunst und das schone Heim, Munich, May, 1955.

MARCHIORI G.: *Santomaso*. Catalogue for the VII Quadriennale, Rome, 1955-56.

APOLLONIO U.: *Elementi della natura in un pittore astratto*. (Nature as a factor in the painting of an abstract painter). Quadrum, n. 3, Bruxelles, 1957.

MARCHIORI G.: *Tempere di Santomaso.* (Santomaso's work in tempera). Catalogue for the show at the Segno Gallery, Rome, December 7-21, 1957.

ANTONIO CORPORA

Born in Tunis, 1909; now resides in Rome. He first studied in Tunis, and then in Florence and Paris. In 1939 he had a one-man show at the Gallery del Milione in Milan. In 1945 he was one of the founders of the Neo-Cubist Roman Group, and the Fronte Nuovo delle Arti *(New Art Front), and the* Gruppo degli otto pittori italiani *(the group of eight). His work has been shown in all the most important art exhibits both in Italy and abroad. He won the Paris Prize in 1951, and others at the Biennales of 1950, 1952, 1956, and at the Rome Quadriennale 1955-56. His works are on show at the National Gallery of Modern Art in Rome, the Paris Museum of Modern Art, the Stättisches Museum of Leverkusen, the Museum of Fine Arts of La Chaux-des-Fonds, The Carnegie Art Institute of Pittsburgh, the St. Louis Museum, as well as in many private collections both in Europe and in the United States.*

Writings by Corpora:

Corpora has also worked as a journalist and has published a novel. Only such writings of his that have a particular bearing on problems of painting and art in general are listed here.

L'arte e il pubblico. (Art and the public). La Fiera Letteraria, Rome, July 11, 1946.
Della Tecnica in arte. (Of technique in art). La Fiera Letteraria, Rome, October 3, 1946.
Arte Francese d'Oggi a Roma. (French art of today in Rome). La Fiera Letteraria, Rome, October 17, 1946.
Arte Francese d'Oggi a Roma (II). (French art of today in Rome (II)). La Fiera Letteraria, Rome, October 24, 1946.
Colloqui con Fougeron. (Talks with Fougeron). La Fiera Letteraria, Rome, May 1, 1947.
Lettera a Raffaele Castello. (Letter to Raffaele Castello). La Fiera Letteraria, Rome, September 4, 1947.
Caratteri essenziali della pittura moderna. (Essential characteristics of modern painting). La Fiera Letteraria, Rome, December, 1947.
Sconfitte e vittorie di una generazione. (Defeats and victories of a generation). Commentari, vol. I, Rome, 1955.
Dichiarazione. (Declaration). Painting in Postwar Italy, catalogue for the show organized by Columbia University, New York, 1958.
L'arte d'oggi è non figurativa. (Today's art is not figurative). Il Punto, Rome, March 1, 1958.

Bibliography:

DEL MASSA A.: *Corpora.* L'illustrazione Toscana, n. 3, Florence, 1930.
CARRIERI R.: *Corpora alla Galleria del Milione.* (Corpora at the Galleria del Milione). L'Illustrazione Italiana, Milan, June 18, 1939.
VENTURI L.: *Corpora.* (With a note of Libero De Libero, Edizioni del Cortile, Rome, 1948).
DEGAND L.: *Corpora.* Art d'Aujourd'hui, Boulogne sur Seine, 1950.
ZERVOS C.: *Corpora.* Editions du Centre d'Art Italien, Paris, 1952.
ZERVOS C.: *Corpora.* Cahiers d'Art, n. 1, Paris 1952.
GUEGEN P.: *Corpora.* XX Siècle, Paris, 1952.
GROHMAN P.: *Corpora.* Neue Zeitung, Berlin, November 5, 1953.
VENTURI L.: *Corpora.* Commentari, vol. I, Rome, 1955.
BALLO G.: *Corpora.* With an introduction by Lionello Venturi and a biographical note by Nello Ponente. Edizioni Mediterranee, Rome, 1956.
ARGAN G. C.: *Corpora.* Introduction to the catalogue for the show at the XXVIII Biennale, Venice, 1956.
ZERVOS C.: *Corpora.* With essays by Lionello Venturi, André Chastel, Léon Degand, Giulio C. Argan, Pierre Francastel, Editions des Cahiers d'Art, Paris, 1957.
CHASTEL A.: *Corpora.* Le Monde, Paris, June 28, 1957.
ELGAR F.: *Corpora.* Carrefour, Paris, July 24, 1957.
PONENTE N.: *Appunti sui quadri recenti di Corpora.* (Notes on recent paintings by Corpora). Commentari, vol. I, Rome, 1958.
ARGAN G. C.: *Corpora.* Introduction to the catalogue for the show at the Springer Gallery, Berlin, June, 1958.
CRISPOLTI L.: *L'ultimo Corpora.* (Corpora's latest style). Notizie, Turin, July, 1958.
VENTURI L.: *Corpora.* Introduction to the catalogue for the show at the Kleemann Gallery, New York, November, 1958.
RESTANY P.: Introduction to the catalogue for the show at the Galleria Blu, Milan, April, 1959.

AFRO

Born in Udine, 1912, now lives in Rome. He studied at the Art Lyceum in Venice and has exhibited in the most important exhibitions both in Italy and abroad; and has had many one-man shows both in Europe and in America. He won the first prize for an Italian painter at the Venice Biennale, 1956. His works are hung in the National Gallery of Modern Art in Rome, the International Gallery of Modern Art in Venice, the Rivoltella Museum in Trieste, and in the museum of Helsinki, La Chaux-des-Fonds, Detroit, St. Louis, Brooklyn, the Albright Gallery of Buffalo, the Museum of Modern Art of New York, the Barnes Foundation, Merion, Pennsylvania, the Solomon Guggenheim Foundation of New York, the Carnegie Institute of Pittsburgh, the Tate Gallery of London, and in many other public and private collections, in Italy and abroad.

Writings by Afro:

Dichiarazione. (Declaration). The New Decade, edited by Andrew Carnduff Ritchie, The Museum of Modern Art, New York, 1955.
Le ragioni dell'arte giovane. (A justification for the new art). Libertà della Cultura, Rome, May-June, 1955.
Arshile Gorky. Introduction for the show of Gorky's drawings at the Obelisco Gallery, Rome February, 1957.

Bibliography:

DE LIBERO L.: *Pitture di Afro.* (Paintings by Afro). Introduction for the show to the Cometa Gallery, Rome, April, 1936.
DE LIBERO L.: *Afro.* Edizioni della Cometa, Rome, 1946.
  VENTURI L.: *Afro.* Commentari, vol. III, Rome, 1954.
MARCHIORI G.: *Afro oggi.* (Afro today). Letteratura n. 13-14, Rome, 1955.
VENTURI L.: *Afro.* Catalogue for the show at the Catherine Viviano Gallery, New York, April-May, 1955.
VENTURI L.: *Afro.* Arts and Architecture, Los Angeles, May, 1955.
ASHTON D.: *Synthesists.* Arts and Architecture, Los Angeles, September 1955.
RITCHIE A. C.: *Afro.* Introduction to the catalogue for the XXVIII Biennale, Venice, 1956.

APOLLONIO U.: *Appunto per Afro.* (Note on Afro). I quattro Soli, Turin, May-August, 1956.
CALVESI M.: *Afro.* Comunità, Milan, October, 1956.
EFRATI C.: *Afro.* Arti Visive, n. 5, Rome, 1956.
APOLLONIO U.: *Afro.* Quadrum, n. 2, Bruxelles, 1956.
PONENTE N.: *Afro.* Taccuino delle Arti, n. 15, Rome, 1957.
FEZZI E.: *Afro.* Prisme des Arts, Paris, March, 1957.

BRUNO CASSINARI

Born in Piacenza, 1912, now resides in Milan. As a boy he was apprenticed to a goldsmith, and later became a student, at the Gazzola Art School. At seventeen he moved to Milan, where he attended courses at the Brera Academy. In 1940 his work was shown for the first time at the Corrente Gallery, and already by 1941 he had won the Bergamo Prize. Since then he has won a number of other prizes, among them ex aequo *the one for an Italian painter at the Venice Biennale, 1952, and the first prize of the Rome Quadriennale, 1955-56. In 1946 Cassinari became one of the founders of the* Nuova Secessione Artistica, (*new artistic secession*) *but he withdrew his support from this movement when it developed into the* Fronte Nuovo delle Arti (*New Art Front*). *He has traveled a great deal in France, spending most of his time in Paris and Antibes. His works are hung in the National Gallery of Modern Art in Rome, in that of Turin, and in many other museums and private and public collections both in Italy and abroad.*

There are no writings by Cassinari himself, except for a reply to a survey published by the Milan edition of L'Unità, October 29, 1945.

Bibliography:

LABÒ G.: *Cassinari.* Corrente di Vita Giovanile Milan, April 15, 1939.
VITTORINI E.: *Cassinari.* Introduction for the show at the Corrente Gallery, Milan, 1940.
PIOVENE G.: *Cassinari.* La Nuova Europa, Rome, August 12, 1945.
SCIALOJA T.: *Cassinari.* L'Immagine, n. 2, Rome, 1947.
BRANDI C.: *Cassinari.* L'Immagine, n. 12, Rome, 1949.

De Grada R.: *Birolli, Cassinari, Morlotti, Treccani.* Edizioni del Milione, Milan, 1950.

Degenhart B.: *Cassinari.* Die Presse, Munich, December 2, 1951.

Vitali L.: *Cassinari.* Catalogue for the XXVI Biennale, Venice, 1952.

Valsecchi M.: *Cassinari.* La Fiera Letteraria, Rome, September 21, 1952.

Scialoja T.: *Cassinari, pittore metafisico.* (Cassinari as a metaphysical painter). Letteratura, n. 3, Rome, 1953.

Russoli F.: *Cassinari.* Bollettino della Galleria del Milione, n. 8, Milan, May, 1955.

Venturi L.: *Cassinari.* Commentari, vol. IV, Rome, 1955.

Valsecchi M.: *Cassinari.* Edizioni del Milione, Milan, 1955.

Russoli F.: *Cassinari-Disegni.* (Cassinari-Drawings). Edizioni Cappelli, Bologna, 1955.

Ponente N.: *Cassinari.* Taccuino delle Arti, n. 18, Rome, 1957.

Ponente N.: *Cassinari.* Introduction for the show at the La Bussola Gallery, Rome, April, 1958.

GIULIO TURCATO

Born in Mantova, 1912, he now resides in Rome. He studied in Venice. After the war he took part actively in those groups that were working towards the development of a new Italian art style. He worked with the Neo-Cubism group, and later with the movement Forma *(form) comprising young abstract artists; later still he was part of the* Fronte Nuovo delle Arti *(New Art Front), and finally in 1952, at Venice, he exhibited with the* Gruppo degli Otto Pittori Italiani *(the group of eight). His work has been shown in the most important art exhibitions in Italy and abroad, and he has had various one-man shows in several towns of Europe. His work was exhibited at the Sao Paulo Biennale, 1957, and at the Guggenheim Award Show, New York, 1958. His works are hung in the National Gallery of Modern Art in Rome, in the museum of Sao Paulo, and in many other public and private collections in Italy and abroad.*

Writings:

Crisi della Pittura. (The crisis in painting). Forma I, Rome, March 15, 1947.

Tre Biscotti. (Three biscuits). Pittori che scrivono, edited by Leonardo Sinisgalli, Milan, 1954, page 217.

Tempi di riscatto. (Years of redemption). Realismo, n. 2, Milan, March-April, 1955.

Pensieri sul disegno. (Thoughts on drawing). Civiltà delle Macchine, Rome, 1956.

Un pittore giudica l'architettura. (A painter looks at architecture). Architettura n. 12, Rome, October, 1956.

Dichiarazione. (Declaration). Painting in Post-war Italy, catalogue for the show organized by Columbia University, New York, 1958.

Le correnti dell'astrattismo. (Currents in abstract painting). Il Punto, Rome, April 26, 1958.

Bibliography:

Maltese C.: *Giulio Turcato.* Prima Mostra del Fronte Nuovo delle Arti, Milan, 1947.

Maselli E.: *Consagra, Corpora, Turcato.* L'Avanti, Rome, February 15, 1949.

Maltese C.: *Turcato al secolo.* (Turcato at the Secolo Gallery). L'Unità, Rome, April 14, 1950.

Moretti U.: *Turcato.* La Libertà, Rome, April 18, 1950.

Trombadori A.: *Turcato.* Introduction for the one-man show at the Naviglio Gallery, Milan, October 28-November 6, 1953.

Villa E.: *Pittura di Giulio Turcato.* (Giulio Turcato's painting). Arti Visive, n. 1, Roma, 1955.

Mezio A.: *Una presentazione per Turcato.* (Introduction to Turcato). Catalogue for the show at the Tartaruga Gallery, Rome, March, 1955.

Brandi C.: *Turcato, neon fra le foglie morte.* (Turcato, a neon light among dead foliage). Cronache, Rome, March 5, 1955.

Russoli F.: *Le favole astratte di Turcato.* (The abstract fables of Turcato). Settimo Giorno, Milan, January 2, 1957.

Venturi L.: *Giulio Turcato.* Commentari, vol. II, Rome, 1957.

Vivaldi L.: *Giulio Turcato.* L'Esperienza Moderna, n. 2, Rome, 1957.

Ponente N.: *Ripresa di Turcato.* (Another Turcato show). Avviso, Milan, January 31, 1958.

Bucarelli P.: *Giulio Turcato.* Introduction to the catalogue for the XXIX Biennale, Venice, 1958.

Ponente N.: *Giulio Turcato.* Letteratura n. 33-34, Rome, 1958.

TOTI SCIALOJA

Born in Rome, and a resident of that city. He started to paint in 1940, and had his first show in Turin, 1945. Since then he has exhibited regularly in various Italian cities and in New York, and has also taken part in the chief Italian and international art exhibits. From 1943 to 1956 he worked on the stage designs and costumes for a number of ballets and operas in Rome, Venice, Florence, Palermo, Sao Paulo and other cities. In 1955 he won the fifth prize in the Carnegie International Institute. His works are hung in numerous private and public collections in Italy and abroad, in the National Gallery of Modern Art in Rome, the International Gallery in Venice, the Carnegie Institute in Pittsburgh, and in the Denver Art Museum.

Writings:

This list does not make any mention either of articles or of critical essays published between 1942 and 1953 in such reviews as "Il Selvaggio," "Mercurio", "L'Immagine", "Il Mondo" (of Florence), "Letteratura", "Ulisse", etc. nor of his creative writings also published in book form; the following works are those in which the painter discusses painting in general and his own in particular.

Dialogo triste. (A sad dialogue). Il Selvaggio, Rome, December, 1942.

Attualità del nostro decadentismo pittorico. (The acute decadence of painting to-day). Mercurio, Rome, May, 1945.

Le ragioni dell'arte giovane. (A justification of the new art movement). Libertà della Cultura, Rome, May-June, 1955.

Un pittore giudica l'architettura. (A painter looks at architecture). Rome, July-August, 1955.

Per Gorky. (On Gorky). Arti Visive, n. 6-7, Rome, 1957.

Documenti di una nuova figurazione. (Data on a new form of expression). L'Esperienza Moderna, n. 2, Rome, 1957.

Dichiarazione. (Declaration). Painting in Post-war Italy), Catalogue for the show organized by Columbia University, New York, 1958.

Tre pagine di giornale. (Three pages from a diary 1958). L'Esperienza Moderna, n. 5, Rome, 1959.

Bibliography:

BRANDI C.: *Quattro artisti fuori strada.* (Four off-beat artists). Catalogue for the group show at the Secolo Gallery, Rome, March, 1947.

MASCIOTTA M.: *Motivi della pittura di Toti Scialoja.* (The subject matter of Toti Scialoja's painting). Letteratura, n. I, Rome, January-February, 1954, page 55-56.

BERTOLUCCI A.: *Toti Scialoja.* Bollettino della Galleria del Milione, n. 10, Milan, October, 1954.

PASOLINI P. P.: *Toti Scialoja.* Catalogue for the show at the Teatro Gallery, Parma, May, 1955.

GENDEL M.: *Scialoja paints a picture.* Art News, New York, June-August, 1955, pages 42-45, 69-70.

ASHTON D.: *Synthesists.* Arts and Architecture, Los Angeles, September, 1955, Page 6-8.

WASHBURN G. B.: *A labor of love.* Carnegie Magazine, Pittsburgh, November, 1955.

MARCHIORI G.: *Toti Scialoja.* Catalogue for the VII Quadriennale, Rome, 1955-56.

VENTURI L.: *Toti Scialoja.* Commentari, vol. II, Rome, 1956.

DEVREE H.: *About art and artists.* The New York Times, New York, October, 1956.

P. T. (PARKER TYLER).: *Toti Scialoja.* Art News, New York, November 9, 1956.

BERTOLUCCI A.: *Mostra romana di Afro, Burri, Scialoja.* (Roman exhibition of Afro, Burri, Scialoja). La Fiera Letteraria, Rome, March, 3, 1957.

PONENTE N.: *Cronache Romane.* (Roman news). Letteratura, n. 27-28, Rome, 1957.

SCOTT CHETAM C.: *Toti Scialoja.* Modern Painting, drawing and sculpture collected by L. and J. Pulitzer, Knoedler and Co. New York, 1957.

VENTURI L.: *Toti Scialoja.* Catalogue for the XXIX Biennale, Venice, June, 1958.

FAHLSTROM O.: *Malare i Rom.* (Painters in Rome). Konstrevy, n. 4, Stockholm, 1958.

ANTONIO SCORDIA

Born in Santa Fé, Argentina, 1918, and now resides in Rome. He held his first one-man show in Rome, 1945. For several years since then, he has done drawings for the best Italian literary magazines, He was in South America from 1947 to 1949, and exhibited both in Buenos Aires and in Cordoba. On his return to Europe, after a long stay in Paris and London, he took up permanent residence in Rome, where he has had several one-man shows; he has also taken part in the most important exhibitions of Italian art both in Italy and abroad, and in 1957 was hung at the Biennale of Sao Paulo. His works are hung in the National Gallery of Modern Art in Rome, the Gallery of Modern Art in Buenos Aires, the National Gallery of Victoria, Melbourne, and in many public and private collections in Europe and abroad.

Writings:

Risposta ad un invito. (Reply to an invitation). Pittori che scrivono, edited by Leonardo Sinisgalli, Milan, 1954.

Visita alla F.M.I. (A visit to the F.M.I.). Text and drawings, Civiltà delle Macchine, Rome, September, 1957.

Dichiarazione. (Declaration). Painting in Post-war Italy, catalogue for the show organized by Columbia University, New York, 1958.

Bibliography

MASELLI E.: *Scordia.* Introduction for the show at the Galleria del Secolo, Rome, June, 1945.

SCIALOJA T.: *Quattro pittori nuovissimi.* (Four of the latest painters). Mercurio, Rome, July, 1945.

GALLUPPI E.: *Antonio Scordia.* La Fiera Letteraria, Rome, April 10, 1947.

BRUGHETTI R.: *Scordia.* Cabalgada, Buenos Aires, April, 1948.

SCIALOJA T.: *Scordia.* Introduction for the one-man show at the Il Pincio Gallery, Rome, December 18, 1951.

MUJCA LANEZ M.: *Scordia.* Introduction for the one-man show at the Bonino Gallery, Buenos Aires, September-October, 1954.

CALVESI M.: *Scordia.* Introduction in the catalogue for the VII Quadriennale, Rome, 1955-56.

CALVESI M.: *Scordia.* Introduction for the show of drawings at the XXVIII Biennale, Venice, 1956.

COATES R. M.: *The Art Gallery - The Quadriennale.* The New Yorker, New York, January, 1956.

MASCIOTTA M.: *Gli Italiani alla Biennale.* (Italian painters at the Biennale. Letteratura, n. 23, Rome, 1956.

PONENTE N.: *Antonio Scordia.* Letteratura, n. 27-28, Rome, 1957.

VENTURI L.: *Antonio Scordia.* Commentari, vol. III, Rome, 1957.

PONENTE N.: *Tempere di Scordia.* (Scordia's work in tempera). Introduction for the show at the Il Segno, Gallery, Rome, April, 1958.

CALVESI M.: Introduction for the one-man show at the Attico Gallery, Rome, May 1959.

EMILIO VEDOVA

Born in Venice, 1919, and a resident of that city. Vedova is a self-taught artist; he was active in the Corrente *movement from 1942 onward, later on he was one of the founders of the* Fronte Nuovo delle Arti *(New Art Front), and in 1952 he exhibited with the* Gruppo degli otto pittori italiani *(the group of eight). He has had many one-man shows in various cities, both in Europe and in America, and his work has been shown in all the most important artistic exhibitions. In 1958 the Polish Government organized in Warsaw a large retrospective exhibition of his work, dating from 1937 to the present. He has won various prizes, among them the Guggenheim award of 1956. His works are hung in the National Gallery of Modern Art in Rome, in Venice, Turin, Trieste, La Spezia, the museum of Sao Paulo, Araraquara, the Kunsthistoriches Museum of Vienna, the Stuttgart Museum and in many other public and private collections in Italy and abroad.*

Writings

Parole dette. (Statements). Vento di Montagna, Venice, 1946.

Parole dette per strada. (Statements along the road). Oltre Guernica, n. 3, Milan, 1946.

Autopresentazione. (Introduction to his own work). Catalogue for his one-man show at the Piccola Galleria, Venice, 1946.

Dipingere un naso non è così semplice. (Painting a nose is not an easy task). Il Mattino del Popolo, Venice, February 1, 1948.

Eresia di Vedova (da una lettera ad un amico). (Vedova's heresy. From a letter to a friend). Cronache Veneziane, Venice, November 13, 1949.

Fine del Fronte Nuovo delle Arti. (The end of the new art front). Cronache Veneziane, Venice, 1950.

Lettera dal Brasile .(A letter from Brazil). I Quattro Soli, Turin, June, 1954.

Infinite porte da aprire. (A number of doors remaining to be opened). Quaderni di San Giorgio, n. 2, Venice, 1954.

Dal Diario. (Extracts from a diary). Letteratura, n. 29, Rome, 1957.

Bibliography

GUIDA G.: *Un artista di 16 anni: Emilio Vedova.* (Emilio Vedova: artist from the age of sixteen). L'Illustrazione Vaticana, Rome, August 16, 1937.

MARCHIORI G.: *Emilio Vedova.* Catalogue for the show to the Pioppo Gallery, Mantova, 1945.

APOLLONIO U.: *Vedova.* portfolio with five original drawings. Cavallino Editions, Venice, 1950.

MARCHIORI G.: *Emilio Vedova.* Edizioni Arti, Venice, 1951.

APOLLONIO U.: *Peintres italiens d'aujourd'hui: Emilio Vedova.* (Italian painters of to-day: Emilio Vedova). Cahiers d'Art, Paris, June, 1953.

MARCHIORI G.: *Vedova.* Arti Visive, Rome, 1954.

ARGAN G. C.: *Vedova.* Introduction to the catalogue for the XXVIII Biennale, Venice, 1956.

VENTURI L.: *Emilio Vedova.* Commentari, vol. I, Rome, 1956.

ARGAN G. C.: *Emilio Vedova Premio Guggenheim Foundation.* (Emilio Vedova, prize Guggenheim Foundation). Quattro Soli, n. 1, Turin, 1956.

BRANZI S.: *Emilio Vedova.* Scritti di storia dell'arte in onore di Lionello Venturi, Publisher De Luca, Rome, 1956, pages 239-246.

HAFTMANN W.: *Emilio Vedova.* Introduction to the catalogue for the show at the Springer Gallery, Berlin, 1957.

MAZZARIOL G.: *Emilio Vedova.* Quadrum, n. 4, Bruxelles, 1957.

CRISPOLTI E.: *I manifesti universali di Vedova.* (Vedova's manifestoes). Civiltà delle Macchine n. 4, Rome, 1957.

PONENTE N.: *Emilio Vedova.* Letteratura n. 29, Rome, 1957.

STARZYNSKI J. - MARCHIORI G. - ARGAN G. C.: *Emilio Vedova.* Introduction to the catalogue for the show organized by the central bureau Wystaw Artystcznych, Warsaw, 1958.

172

BIBLIOGRAPHY

ARGAN G. C.: *Pittura italiana e Cultura europea.* (Italian painting and European culture). Prosa no. 3, Milan, 1946.

CAIROLA S.: *Arte italiana del nostro tempo.* (Italian art in our times). Bergamo, 1946.

BRANDI C.: *Europeismo e autonomia di cultura della pittura moderna italiana.* (European aspect and cultural autonomy in modern Italian painting). L'Immagine, vol. I. II. III., Rome, 1947.

Catalogo Prima mostra del Fronte Nuovo delle Arti. (Catalogue of the first show of the new art front). Galleria della Spiga, Milan, 1947.

VENTURI L.: *La pittura contemporanea.* (Contemporary painting). Milan, 1947.

ARGAN G. C.: *Peinture italienne et peinture européenne.* (Italian and European painting). Les Arts plastiques, n. 5-6, Paris, 1948.

MARCHIORI G.: *Il fronte nuovo delle arti.* (The New Art Front). Catalogue for the XXIV Biennale, Venice, 1948.

MARCHIORI G.: *Arte Moderna all'Angelo.* (Modern art at the Angelo Gallery), Venice, 1948.

GHIRINGHELLI G.: *Pittura moderna italiana.* (Modern Italian painting). Turin, 1949.

SOBY J. T. - BARR A. H. jr.: *XX century Italian art.* The Museum of Modern Art, New York, 1949.

VENTURI L.: *The new Italy arrives in America.* Art News, New York, summer 1949.

Italienische Malerei der Gegenwart. (Contemporary Italian Painting). Catalogue for the show at the Italian cultural institute, Vienna, with an introduction by Giulio Carlo Argan, Vienna, December 1949 - January 1950,

APOLLONIO U.: *Pittura Italiana moderna.* (Modern Italian painting). Venice, 1950.

CARRIERI R.: *Pittura e scultura di avanguardia in Italia.* (Avant-garde painting and sculpture in Italy). Milan, 1950.

Quelques Jeunes. (Some young artists). Cahiers d'Art. Volume dedicated to Italian contemporary art. Paris, 1950.

ZERVOS C.: *Vue d'ensemble sur l'Art Italien moderne.* (A general view on Italian modern art). Cahiers d'Art. Volume dedicated to Italian contemporary art, Paris, 1950.

Panorama dell'arte italiana. (Panorama of Italian art). Edited by Valsecchi M. and Apollonio U., Turin, 1950 and 1951.

Italian artists of to-day. Exhibition of Italian contemporary art in Sweden, Norway, Denmark, Finland, 1951.

DEGAND L.: *L'art d'avangarde en Italie.* (Avant-garde art in Italy). Art d'Aujourd'hui, Boulogne sur Seine, January 1952.

VENTURI L.: *Otto pittori italiani: Afro, Birolli, Corpora, Moreni, Morlotti, Santomaso, Turcato, Vedova.* (Eight Italian painters: Afro, Birolli, Corpora, Moreni, Morlotti, Santomaso, Turcato, Vedova). Published by De Luca, Rome, 1952.

APOLLONIO U.: *Premier bilan de l'art actuel.* (A first balance-sheet of modern art.) Paris, 1953.

Arte italiana d'oggi. (Italian art of today). Catalogue for the show at Athens, March 20 - April 19, 1953, with introductions by Giovanni Ponti and Umbro Apollonio.

Junge italienische Kunst. (Young Italian art). Catalogue for the show at the Kunsthaus in Zurich, November 21, 1953 - January 10, 1954.

ARCANGELI F.: *Gli ultimi naturalisti.* (The last naturalists). Paragone, n. 59, Florence, 1954.

Pittura d'oggi. (Today's painting). Edited by Michelangelo Masciotta. Florence, 1954.

Arte italiana contemporanea. (Contemporary Italian art). Catalogue edited by Nello Ponente, with an introduction by Palma Bucarelli, Barcelona and Madrid, 1955.

DORAZIO P.: *La fantasia dell'arte nella vita moderna.* (Art and imagination in modern life). Rome, 1955.

PONENTE N.: *Un demi-siècle d'art en Italie - Positions alternatives de la culture artistique italienne.* (A half century of art in Italy - Alternative positions in Italian artistic culture). Cahiers d'Art, XXX year, Paris, 1955.

RITCHIE A. C.: *The new decade.* The Museum of Modern Art, New York, 1955.

ARGAN G. C.: *Studi e note.* (Studies and notes). Rome, 1956.

BALLO G.: *Pittori italiani dal futurismo ad oggi.* (Italian painters from Futurism to the present time). Edizioni Mediterranee, Rome, 1956.

DEGENHART B.: *Italienische Zeichner der Gegenwart* (Contemporary Italian draughtsmen). Berlin, 1956.

LAVAGNINO E.: *L'Arte Moderna.* (Modern art). U.T.E.T., Turin, 1956.

RUSSOLI F.: *Presence de l'art italien.* (Affirmation of Italian art). XX Siècle, Paris, 1956.

ARCANGELI F.: *Una situazione non improbabile.* (A situation likely to be true). Paragone, n. 85, Florence, 1957.

Artistas Italianos de hoje. (Italian artists of today). Catalogue for the IV Biennale, Sao Paulo.

Diez anos de pintura Italiana. (Ten years of Italian painting). Traveling show in South America, organized by the Venice Biennale, Museum of Fine Arts, Caracas, January 27 - February 17, 1957.

DROAZIO P.: *Recent Italian painting and its environment.* The World of abstract art, New York, 1957.

PALLUCCHINI R.: *L'Art contemporain en Italie.* (Contemporary art in Italy). Prisme des Arts, n. 12, Paris, 1957.

Pittori moderni della collezione Cavellini. (Modern painters in the Cavellini collection). Catalogue for the exhibition at the National Gallery of Modern Art, edited by Giovanni Carandente with an introduction by Palma Bucarelli, Rome, May-September, 1957.

SAUVAGE T.: *Pittura Italiana del dopoguerra.* (Painting in post-war Italy). Published by Schwarz, Milan, 1957.

Painting in post-war Italy. Catalogue for the exhibition at Columbia University, with an introduction by Lionello Venturi, New York, 1958.

Pittori tedeschi e italiani contemporanei. (Contemporary German and Italian painters). Catalogue for the exhibition at the National Gallery of Modern Art; introductions by Palma Bucarelli and Curt Schweicher; essays on Italian painters by Nello Ponente, Rome April 10 - May 8, 1958.

CAVELLINI A.: *Arte astratta. Poesia e vita difficile di una tendenza artistica.* (Poetry of an artistic trend and difficulties it encounters). Edizioni della Conchiglia, Milan, 1958.

MODESTI R.: *Pittura Italiana contemporanea.* (Contemporary Italian painting). Vallardi, Milan, 1958.

ARGAN G. C. - PONENTE N.: *Art since 1945*, English edition, London, 1958.

PONENTE N.: *Saggi e profili*, published by De Luca, Rome, 1958.

VENTURI L.: *Peintres italiens d'aujourd'hui.* (Italian painters today). Aujourd'hui, Boulogne-sur-Seine, December, 1958.

PONENTE N.: *Situation de la peinture italienne.* (Position of Italian painting). Aujourd'hui, Boulogne-sur-Seine, December 1958.

PLATES

Turcato

Scialoja

Scordia

Vedova

INDEX

ISTITUTO GRAFICO TIBERINO DI LUIGI DE LUCA - ROMA - PRINTED IN ITALY